Cosmic Teachings of a Lama

THE KALACHAKRA: THE WHEEL OF TIME

COSMIC TEACHINGS OF A LAMA

GNOSIS, SCIENCE, AND THE BUDDHIST AND EGYPTIAN MYSTERIES

Samael Aun Weor

THELEMA PRESS
2007

Cosmic Teachings of a Lama
Christmas Message 1969-1970
A Thelema Press Book / 2007

Originally published as "Mi Regreso al Tibet," 1970

This Edition © 2007 Thelema Press

ISBN 978-1-934206-21-8

Thelema Press is a non-profit organization delivering to
humanity the teachings of Samael Aun Weor. All proceeds go to
further the distribution of these books. For more information,
visit our website.

www.gnosticteachings.org
www.gnosticradio.org
www.gnosticschool.org
www.gnosticstore.org
www.gnosticvideos.org
www.thelemapress.com

Contents

Illustrations

Chapter 1

The Seven Eternities

The Abstract Absolute Space is the *causa causorum* of everything that is, has been, and shall be.

The profound and joyful space is certainly the incomprehensible "Seity," which is the ineffable, mystical root of the seven cosmos. It is the mysterious origin of all that we know as Spirit, matter, universes, suns, worlds, etc.

"That," which is divine, the space of happiness, is the tremendous reality beyond the universe and Gods.

"That" has no dimension, yet, indeed, it is what is, what always has been, and what always will be. It is the life that intensely palpitates within each atom and within each sun.

Let us now refer to the great ocean of the Spirit: how can we define it? Certainly, He is Brahma, who is the first differentiation or modification of "That." The Gods and humans tremble when before "That."

Is "That" Spirit? Indeed, I tell you that it is not. Is "That" matter? Truly, I tell you that it is not.

"That" is the root of the Spirit and of matter, yet it is neither Spirit nor matter.

"That" transcends the laws of numbers, measurement, and weight, it transcends quantity, any side, front, behind, above, below, etc.

"That" has reality beyond thought, word, and action.

"That" is not of time and it is beyond silence and sound, even beyond the ears to perceive it.

"That" is the immutable within a profound, divine abstraction. It is light that has never been created by any God, nor by any human. "That" is what has no name.

Brahma is Spirit; yet "That" is not Spirit. The Absolute, the Unmanifested One, is uncreated light.

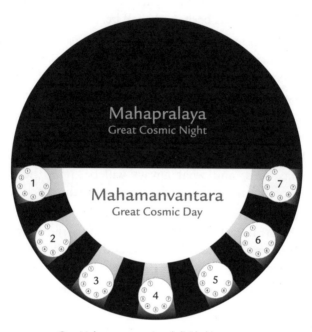

One Mahamanvatara is subdivided into seven
Manvantaras. Further, one Manvantara is
subdivided into seven periods or epochs.

Where was the raw matter of the Great Work? It is evident that it was reposing before the dawn of creation within the profound bosom of the Abstract Absolute Space.

Indeed, the primordial matter becomes like the soul of the Unique One, the living noumenon of any substance. It is an undifferentiated Cosmic Matter.

Ancient wisdom states that when the Great Night (which is what the Hindus call Pralaya or dissolution of the universe) arrives, then, Brahma, the Father, the Ocean of the Universal Spirit of Life, submerges Himself within the Absolute Abstract Space for seven eternities.

The seven eternities signify "EVOS," or totally defined, clear, and precise periods of time.

It has been stated unto us that a Mahakalpa, a Great Age, a Cosmic Day, has indeed a total of 311,040,000,000,000 years. It is obvious that a Mahapralaya, a Cosmic Night, is equivalent to the same quantity of time.

Space is filled with universes. Thus, while some systems of worlds are coming out of their profound night, others are arriving to their dusk. At one place there exists cradles, and at another sepulchres.

What existed before the dawn of this Great Day within which we live, move, and have our Being? The *Rig Veda* answers with the following:

> *Nor Aught nor Nought existed;*
> *Yon bright sky was not,*
> *Nor heaven's broad roof outstretched above.*
> *What covered all? what sheltered ? what concealed ?*
> *Was it the water's fathomless abyss ?*
> *There was not death - yet there was nought immortal,*
> *There was no confine betwixt day and night;*
> *The only One breathed breathless by itself,*
> *Other than It there nothing since has been.*
> *Darkness there was, and all at first was veiled*
> *In gloom profound - an ocean without light -*
> *The germ that still lay covered in the husk*

Burst forth, one nature, from the fervent heat.
Who knows the secret ? who proclaimed it here?
Whence, whence this manifold creation sprang?
The Gods themselves came later into being -
Who knows from whence this great creation sprang?
That, whence all this great creation came,
Whether Its will created or was mute,
The Most High Seer that is in highest heaven,
He knows it - or perchance even He knows not.
Gazing into eternity...
Ere the foundations of the earth were laid,
Thou wert. And when the subterranean flame
Shall burst its prison and devour the frame
Thou shalt be still as Thou wert before
And knew no change, when time shall be no more.
Oh! endless thought, divine Eternity.

THE SIGN OF THE INFINITE COMPARED TO A TIBETAN *VAJRA*, SYMBOL OF VAJRAYANA BUDDHISM

Chapter 2
People from Other Planets

We, wretched and miserable slugs from the mud of the earth, are perhaps so stubborn that we still need to investigate a little bit more about the possibility of extraterrestrial visitors.

All of the data that we already have; is it perhaps not enough? Are we, for our own disgrace, so dull, slow-witted, and torpid that we do not comprehend that since ancient times we have always been visited by people from other planets?

So, why do they elude us? Why do they run away from us? Why do they not appear at daylight? Would we, perhaps, not do the same thing if we were to come face to face with a tribe of cannibals?

People from other planets know very well that we are not meek sheep. Therefore, instead of falling into our fratricidal feline claws, they prefer to furtively disappear into the starry heaven.

What would the great leaders of the earth do with these type of cosmic ships? This is not difficult to guess. How frightful those "UFOs" would be if they were equipped with atomic bombs!

So, to be sent to jail without any motive, without any reason, or to become a guinea pig inside of any laboratory so that others can experiment with you, so that others can extract your glands and inject distinct substances with the purpose of knowing reactions, certainly is not pleasant, whatsoever. Is this not so? It is obvious that the extraterrestrial visitors do not want to take such a risk, therefore they prefer to elude or avoid us.

This does not signify that the people from other planets cannot defend themselves. It is clear, it is evident, that if they already conquered space, they might also be in possession of formidable weapons. Nonetheless, they are not assassins. It is better, by all means, to avoid conflicts.

So, what is going on in regard to us? When are we going to be capable of reciprocating those visitations of our friends, the extraterrestrials?

Certain romantic speculators from the eighteenth and nineteenth centuries thought up the possibility of travelling to the moon, propelling themselves with wings or by means of aerostatic globe systems. It is evident that such fantasies disappeared from the intellectual environment when the limits of our planetary atmosphere was discovered.

The scientific procedures of defined spatial travelling were revived with the marvellous works of Konstantin Eduardovich Tsiolkovsky, within which the cosmic ships are mentioned. In the year 1920, such a cited sage predicted that in a not too faraway future, short radio waves will penetrate within our atmosphere and will become the main method for stellar communications. This prophesy is now being accomplished. Unfortunately, modern scientists still are not capable of interpreting the cosmic messages.

Tsiolkovsky believed that at least on one planet situated in any given place, the human beings would have already reached a technology that would allow them to overcome the law of gravity, thus being able to colonize the universe.

Obviously, regarding this matter, we, the Gnostics go much further beyond. We know very well by means of direct mystical experience that any inoffensive humanity from the infinite cosmic space can give themselves the luxury of travelling to other inhabited planets.

In this modern day and age, the possibility of voyages between solar systems and even fantastic rockets propelled with atomic energy and guided by means of the pressure of light are spoken of.

Presently, very beautiful spatial theories exist. Thus, Russia and the United States of America equally struggle in an arduous manner for the conquest of space.

Lamentably, it becomes evident that in order to arrive at any star similar to the sun that shines upon us, within the period of time of a human lifespan, it is necessary to first break the barrier of the speed of light.

The three-dimensional world exists within the barrier of the speed of light. Therefore, to break this barrier, to indeed transcend it, as a fact, is equivalent to penetrating within the fourth dimension. The fourth dimension is time in itself.

Therefore, the supreme conquest of starry space is not possible if time has not previously been conquered.

We emphatically affirm without any doubt that as long as we remain enclosed within this three-dimensional mould of life, which is determined by the speed of light, the conquest of time is impossible.

It is evident that within the fourth dimension, we can travel throughout time, we can submerge ourselves within a remote past or project ourselves to a distant future. Let us remember that time is circular.

Imagine a cosmic ship having a velocity more than the speed of light taking off from our afflicted planet and going towards some mysterious resplendent sun, situated at a given point, to an incommensurable distance of 137 light years. It is evident and clear that if this ship returned to this valley of tears," always maintaining the same speed during the whole trip, its crew would experience tremendous confusion when finding our planet Earth very well advanced by 270 years in time.

Nevertheless, which cosmic rocket is indeed capable of travelling with a velocity of more than the speed of light?

If indeed the famous rockets traverse to the Moon with a lot of difficulty, and perhaps eventually to Mars, certainly it is evident that the conquest of infinite space with such a system is completely ludicrous.

Purcell, an eminent man of science, seriously analysed the indispensable quantity of energy needed in order to perform an hypothetical roundtrip sidereal voyage towards any shiny star situated some twelve light years away. The specific distinctiveness of this ship is that it must reach the maximum velocity of 99 percent of the speed of light at the middle of its journey, as well as at its departure and its return. Our readers must not forget that light travels at the extraordinary speed of 300,000 kilometres per second [EDITOR: 186,282.397 MILES PER SECOND].

Now, the problem of fuel for this hypothetical voyage must be faced. There is no doubt that in this day and age, the most appropriate source of available energy is the fusion that occurs in the hydrogen bomb, which is when the isotopes, namely tritium and deuterium of the element hydrogen, are wisely combined in order to form helium.

Let us think for a while, dear reader, of the tremendous efficacy of that extraordinary fusion that makes the sun shine. It is evident that within such a formidable nuclear reaction, four nuclei of hydrogen are intelligently combined by immense heat and potent pressure in order to form, indeed, one nucleus of helium.

It is 'obvious that this marvellous, cohesive energy, that integrally maintains the unity of the nucleus of helium, becomes without a doubt, slightly smaller than the energy from the original nucleus of hydrogen. It is stated unto us that after this nuclear reaction, a residue remains which acts in the form of energy free in its movement.

It is evident, certain, and palpable that this special type of liberated energy is powerful, terrific, and tremendous. This is in accordance with the famous equation of Einstein, namely: $E=mc^2$ (energy divided by mass is equal to the square of the speed of light). Therefore, the value of E becomes gigantic in proportion.

Purcell infers in a manner that is certainly very well asserted that with this type of solar fusion, if used in his hypothetical voyage, nothing less than 16,000 million tons of hydrogen would be required in order to move his sidereal ship.

It is clear that for such a voyage of twelve light years, such a cosmic vehicle would have an approximate weight of one hundred tons.

It is logical that such a cosmic ship should be propelled forward when taking off, stopped when arriving, propelled again in order to initiate its return to the planet Earth, and finally stopped again when landing on our planet. So, all of these manoeuvers imply a tremendous consumption of many thousands of millions of tons of fuel. What rocket would be capable of transporting such a quantity of fuel?

Still, the option of obtaining energy by intelligently combining matter with anti-matter is accessible to us. It is already completely demonstrated that if these contrary substances make direct contact, they are mutually destroyed, thus liberating energy in the form of gamma rays.

Indeed, in the name of truth, we have to acknowledge that this is the unique, knowable process through which matter, as well as anti-matter, can be equally transformed into energy.

Evidently, the famous gamma rays are found in the extreme of the short wave, in the electromagnetic spectrum, and obviously can impel a cosmic ship in identical conditions, as if it were impelled by means of the pressure of light.

To every atomic particle there corresponds, as a fact and by its own right, an atomic anti-particle.

It is easy to comprehend that the anti-particle is an image, a reflection, of its original. It is obvious that if the latter is negatively charged like the electron, undoubtedly its particle becomes positive.

Apparently, even though the problem of generating energy in order to propel a cosmic ship in the hypothetical voyage of Purcell has been resolved, it cannot be confirmed.

It is evident that for such a voyage, 406,400 tons of fuel, equally distributed between matter and anti-matter, are urgently needed. Could a ship of 100 tons transport such a quantity of fuel?

We must repeat - and it is important to remember - that we are discussing an hypothetical voyage of just twelve light years away. However, if this hypothetical ship should journey to a point of 50 or 100 light years away, then what would become of this problem of fuel?

In its depth, this certainly is a problem without a solution. Indeed, if we want to conquer space, then we have to focus on this matter from another angle.

We need an authentic scientific revolution. It is urgent to learn how to utilize the solar energy.

This is why Marconi rightly stated, "Where a sunbeam goes, there a human being can also go."

Solar energy and the fourth dimension: these will be the two pillars of the future humanity.

It is necessary to illustrate the fourth vertical. This is only possible by studying the atom very deeply.

Therefore, when the fourth coordinate is outlined, then a new type of tetra-dimensional geometry will be elaborated. It is easy to comprehend that upon this living foundation, a revolutionary four dimensional physics can be created.

Indeed, contemporary physics is regressive, retarded, and reactionary. It is worthless for the conquest of space because it is antiquated and extemporaneous.

When we possess revolutionary, tetra-dimensional physics, then we will be capable of fabricating cosmic ships that can instantaneously cross the barrier of the speed of light. Such cosmic ships can then travel through time with velocities millions of times superior to the speed of light.

Propelled with solar energy, these type of ships would not need to transport fuel of any type and would travel freely throughout the infinite space.

The three-dimensional world is not the "be all and end all." Indeed, it is nothing but a leaf of the tree of life. Let us think of the fourth dimension. Come now, to revolutionize science.

We already passed through the barrier of sound with aeroplanes and ultrasonic capsules. Nevertheless, we still cannot pass through the barrier of the speed of light.

Chapter 3
The Consciousness

When those memories reach me, those ardent effluvia from April and dawn, indeed, when feeling those refreshing drops of dew falling from heaven, I truly suffer for all of the millions of human beings who dream and weep.

My consciousness awakened, I attained illumination. Where was I going, asleep along the rude cliff, rent in twain? I attentively beheld the firmament; it was very high, its tremendous summit with its vertigo enraptured me. Then, I turned my face away from the deep, soaring height. Thus, I saw the Earth, and it was very low.

The Phoenix Bird, when passing by in swift flight, touched me with its wings of immaculate whiteness. Then, filled with fervour, I prayed, knowing that the perfume of prayer always arrives to God.

My prayer was for the sake of the sleepy ones, for those sincere, mistaken ones who dream that they are awakened, for those failed ones who assume they are doing very well.

The sage dreams of the splendid rose of the magical meadow, that when blooming unfolds its delectable petals to the vespertine star of love.

The long-haired bard dreams of the timid, singing rivulet, which when sliding down across the mountain, seems to melt into silver, transfiguring everything into a filigree that runs and passes.

The unfortunate mother dreams of the son whom she lost in the war. She cannot conceive of a harder fate beyond. Thus, she weeps of her broken joy at the foot of his portrait, while the lightning plays with her torture and even lights an iris in every tear.

Faust dreams of his Marguerite with a peaceful, whitened countenance, covered by the exquisite canopy of her golden hair, a cascade of gold that falls over her alabaster shoulders. What a profound abyss within her pupil: perfidious and bluish as a wave!

When in the frightful claws of pain, the wretched intellectual animal dreams of being Brutus, turning asunder the heart of Caesar; or the dreaded Spartacus, devastating the campaign; or Ulysses in his palace at Ithaca, furiously killing the suitors of his wife; or Tell rejecting with his foot the skiff; or Cleopatra seducing Mark Antony; or Cromwell before the supplication of a Monarch; or Mirabeau in the Tabor of nations; or Bolivar with five liberated countries; or Napoleon on the fields of battle.

The one in love dreams of the star rising resplendently in the east, of that long-awaited rendezvous, of the book that she holds in her hands, and of her romantic window.

The offended husband dreams of an obscure dispute and rebellious quarrel; he suffers the unspeakable and even dies in his nightmare.

The lustful one dreams of the lecherous nakedness of the devilish one, who wallows as a pig within the mud of filthiness.

The drunkard dreams of being a wealthy, young, and brave gentleman of great renown, who is valiant in the battle.

Dreaming was Amado Nervo in his *Immovable Beloved* and Victor Hugo in *Les Miserables*. Thus, this lunar type of life is nothing but a web of dreams.

Therefore, those wise elders from the sacred land of the *Vedas* were not mistaken when they asseverated that this world is Maya (illusion).

Ah... if those wretched people would stop dreaming...! Then, how different life would be...!

The Four Gospels insist on the necessity of awakening the consciousness; however, since these are written in code, no one understands them.

Ineffable remembrances reach my memory in these moments. On a given autumn night, I was amiably conversing with an Adept within the superior worlds.

To converse with a Major Brother in the parallel universes of the Superior Dimensions is indeed something impossible for the sleepy ones, for those wretched people who dream. Fortunately, I am awakened...

Varied was the theme of our conversation. The dialogue was developed in synthesis. Litelantes, while listening, was silent... It is obvious that she is also awakened and enjoys accompanying me... She is my priestess-spouse.

Thus, our conversation delectably flowed as a river of gold which slowly flows through the thick jungle under the sun.

The venerable one wanted to set a meeting with me, here, down in this physical world, in this three-dimensional region. To define factors of time and place was necessary. Litelantes complained, "Twelve midnight, and so far from our home, right there in the center of the city of Mexico..."

Useless were her complaints... He and I set that meeting and uttered our pledged word.

The months of autumn passed away... I was awaiting with very much attention for the longed for new year of 1968.

However, everything passes... I did not have to wait for great lengths, as the longed for night soon arrived.

I left my home early, this is how it had to be, since this is the night of too many visits. Thus, I left with anticipation.

A taxi drove me along the road of Tlalpan towards the Zocalo. I had to get off on the 20 de Noviembre street exactly in one of the corners of Plaza de la Constitucion.

I had to pay for the ride... "How much do I owe you?"

"Two pesos, sir..."

"Here it is, take it." The driver received the money without even remotely suspecting anything about the motive of my trip. What can a dreaming one know? Could the poor driver know about my studies? What could I expect from him? He was just another dreaming one driving a taxi. That is all.

Thus, I walked in the very center of El Zocalo. I stopped in front of a great post of steel: this was the mast of our national

PLAZA DE LA CONSTITUCION

flag. This was the exact place for our meeting. I had to first recognize the place, which I did. However, it was not even ten o'clock yet on that night.

I walked, along the Cinco de Mayo street, very slowly... very slowly. Hence, I arrived at El Parque de la Alameda.

The ice from winter that breathes on the hills, where neither hues or aromas are swaying, was descending in refreshing silvery currents covering the withered prairies.

I sat down on a bench in the park. The cold of that winter night was certainly tremendous. Here, there, and everywhere were children, very well covered with winter clothing, happily playing. Austerely, the elders were conversing about things - maybe very serious and grave, or perhaps not so important. The people in love, with luciferian looks of fire, were smiling. Lights of diverse colors were shining, and among those variegated and painteresque human ensembles of the New Year, costumes were not missing. There were jubilant people enjoying themselves when taking a photograph beside the Three Wise Men.

Smoke bursting forth out of the mountain, obscure nostalgia, strange passions, insatiable thirst, immortal tedium, tender and subconscious longing, undefined and infinite yearnings for the impossible is what humanity experiences in those moments.

Many times, walking close to the crystalline fountains, next to the pines, I contemplated beautiful things, globes of various colors, symbolic representations of the old and new year, chariots pulled by the goats of Capricorn, etc, etc, etc.

Time and time again I slowly walked along the Cinco de Mayo avenue. I approached, on many occasions, the mast of our national flag in the bustling center of Plaza de la Constitucion.

I looked with anxiety around the glorious place. I was relatively alone, and the breaking point for me was that the colorful national pavilion of our country (Mexico), namely, the eagle of the spirit, the sacred serpent, and the nopal (cactus) of willpower, was not illuminated.

Obscure Alexanders and Spartacuses! How far you are from comprehending the whole of this, since, in the bloody labors of war, scattered with laurels and disgrace, you were only idols of clay who fell on the ground and were turned into bits and pieces.

Thus, while in sublime absorption, I delved within my own mind, meditating on the mystery of life and death.

Only half of an hour was lacking to reach the time for the mysterious meeting in question. Many times I silently walked over there, between the Zocalo and La Alameda. Suddenly, looking at the clock, I profoundly sighed while saying with a voice that overwhelmed my own self, "Finally, the hour is near."

It was necessary to speed my footsteps a little in order to return once again to the place of the longed for meeting.

The bells of the old metropolitan cathedral resounded at fifteen minutes to twelve midnight, when I anxiously stopped in front of the national flag's mast. Then, I looked around me, inquiring, searching for any sign that could show me the presence of the Master.

Innumerable questions were invading me. Was this Guru incapable of accomplishing our meeting? Maybe this adept did not bring the memory of that commitment to his physical brain?

Finally, oh God of mine! Twelve strokes of the bell announced the New Year, and resounded on the towers of the temple. I then started to feel disappointed, when something unusual happened: I saw three people in front of me. They were a foreign family, maybe North American or British? I did not know.

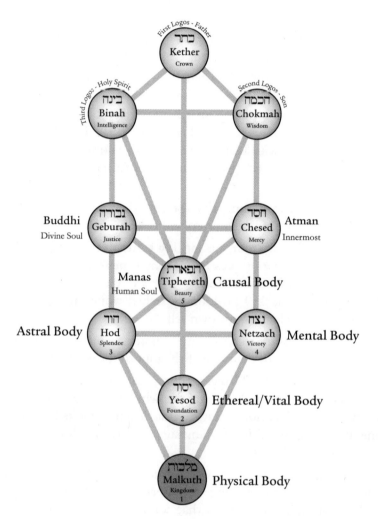

THE MONAD AND THE BODIES OF THE SOUL

The gentleman advanced alone towards me. I attentively observed him. Yes, I know those features, that majestic countenance: he is the Master. He congratulated me, hugged me, and wished for me a complete success for the year 1968. Suddenly, he withdrew.

Nonetheless, I noticed in him something strange: he came to me as a somnambulist, unconscious, as if he was impelled by a force superior to him. This overwhelmed me and made me a little sad.

Could it be that the consciousness of that Master is awakened within the superior worlds, yet asleep in the physical world? Indeed, this is something strange, enigmatic, and profound.

After the encounter with the Master, I did not feel disappointed anymore. I felt joy within my heart.

Happily, I advanced towards the atrium of that old cathedral. Yes, I waited, but soon my son Osiris came for me. He came driving his little fire-colored car. He stopped for a while in order to take me and drive me back home.

"Did the Master accomplish the meeting with you?" This was my son's first question, and since my answer was in the affirmative he clearly was very joyful. Thus, he kept silent.

It is useful to remark that after that event, I had a new interview with the Master within the superior worlds. I thanked him for accomplishing that meeting and I congratulated him. Very happy, that Guru felt satisfied for having had conducted his human personality to the place previously planned.

It is obvious that the Master in himself is what the Hindus name Atman, the Divine Spirit, who is in fusion with his Spiritual Soul (Buddhi).

The Human Soul (Superior Manas), clothed with his terrestrial personality, is what in the mysterious east is wisely denominated "Bodhisattva."

It is easy to comprehend that the man who came to me was the Bodhisattva of the Master.

However, he (the Bodhisattva) came to me asleep... What pain! He was a fallen Bodhisattva... Nonetheless, the Master was able to control him and conduct him as an automaton, as a marionette, to the place of the meeting.

It is not in any way strange that after having fallen, a Bodhisattva (Human Soul of a Master) becomes lamentably submerged within the dream of the unconsciousness.

In ancient times, in those times in which the rivers of the pure water of life were pouring milk and honey, many Masters lived across the face of the earth.

However, with the advent of the age of Kali Yuga, this Black Age in which we disgracefully live, innumerable Bodhisattvas fell. Thus, the lyre of Orpheus fell upon the floor of the temple and broke into pieces.

> *The great ancient Divinity has fallen and collapsed. It reposes over one side, its face against the ground. Nevertheless, the heavenly hierarchies are lifting it.*

Chapter 4
Time

If we attentively observe anything from this Mayavic world in which we live, such as a table, for instance, we discover with mystical astonishment three perfectly defined aspects, namely: length, width, and height.

However, it is evident that in the table used in our example, a specific and totally defined fourth factor exists. I am referring to the concept of time.

How much time has passed since that gleaming table was created by the humble carpenter? Only minutes? Maybe hours? Months? Years?

Length, width, and height are - without any possible doubt (even if these are of a Cartesian type) - the three Euclidean aspects of this three-dimensional world within which, for good or for bad, we live. It is evident that it would be absurd to exclude the fourth factor from our postulations.

Thus, considering time as the fourth dimension, it intrinsically contains two fundamental properties, namely: temporal and spatial.

It is positive, authentic, and undeniable that the chronometric aspect of life is exclusively the unstable surface of the spatial depth.

Many years before, prior to the time of the wise Einstein who surprised the world with his famous Theory of Relativity, any learned person conceived the factor of time as a straight line. However, in this day and age, any intellectual person accepts that such a factor is a curve. Nonetheless, it is also obvious that in this present century, people who think with a medieval mind still exist.

Great modern, intellectual people, utopians by nature, beautifully fantasize when thinking that eternity is also a straight line, time prolonged in an indefinite way.

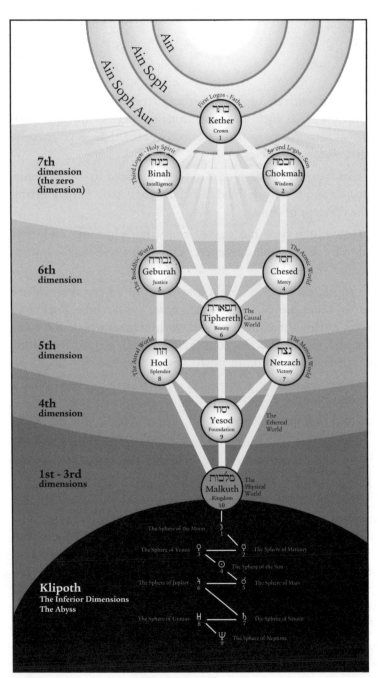

DIMENSIONS AND THE KABBALAH

Revolutionary Gnosticism dialectally teaches that eternity in itself has nothing to do with the concept of time.

The International Gnostic Movement emphatically affirms that a Fifth Dimension exists, known with the solemn name of Eternity.

In accordance with the wise Law of Recurrence, everything in life comes to occur again, just as it happened previously within the vicious circle of time.

Indeed, the times are eternally repeated. Yet, let not time be confused with eternity.

An incessant repetition of events and times exists within the Eternal Now of the great life.

The curve of time perfectly revolves within the perfect circle of eternity; yet, it is evident that these two wheels are different.

That which is beyond these two mysterious circles is the Sixth Dimension, and we must search for the living foundation of any Cosmogenesis within the unknowable Zero Region.

Considering that the wise Einstein already mathematically demonstrated the relativity of time, we can emphasise the idea that the fourth factor (time) of our three-dimensional world, within the Unmanifested Absolute, has no existence.

Before the flaming heart from this solar system of Ors, within which we live, move and have our Being, started to intensely palpitate after the Great Pralaya (Cosmic Night), time did not exist. It was lying asleep within the profound bosom of the Abstract Absolute Space.

If at the end of the Mahamanvantara (Cosmic Day), the seven basic dimensions of the universe remain reduced into a simple mathematical point, which is lost as a drop within the Great Ocean, then it is evident that time ceases to exist.

The worlds, as well as human beings, animals, and plants, are born, grow up, get old, and die. Everything that breathes under the sun has a defined period of time.

The unity of life of any living creature is equivalent, as a fact and by its own right, to every single palpitation of its heart.

Indeed, it has been wisely stated unto us that the whole starry heaven is a system of hearts that intensely palpitate.

It is evident that each palpitation from the worlds is performed every 27,000 years.

The complete life of any world, which sparkles and blazes within the profound bosom of the inalterable infinite, is equivalent to the complete amount of 2,700,000,000 palpitations from the cosmic heart.

The humble insect that only lives for an evening in summer, lives, indeed, as much as any human being or any world, just in a very accelerated way.

It is written with embers of ardent fire that the number of cardiac palpitations for beasts, human beings, and worlds is always the same; however, sometimes more fast or more slow.

Time is extremely relative. Thus, through the stage show of the world, many actors who carry their own chronometer are passing by.

Moreover, secret calculations and esoteric time also exist. This is known by any Adept.

Chapter 5
Darol Froman

The sober mathematical reasoning of Purcell that disqualified the system of cosmic rockets and the sidereal voyages to other solar universes certainly did not discourage everybody. On the contrary, and even if this seems incredible, it stimulated the dishevelled, fantastic idea that possibly, on a not too far off date, the men of science would be able to propel the planet Earth at their own whim and take it out of its orbit in order to transport it to other parts of the galaxy. This dim-witted suggestion was pompously proposed by Darol Froman, technician/ex-director of Los Alamos Scientific Laboratory in New Mexico.

The fundamental energy in order to give concrete form to his monstrous and tenebrous project could be acquired by nuclear reactions of fusion, utilizing the water of the oceans as combustible material.

It is obvious, evident, and noticeable that the maritime bestowal of deuterium, the heavy form of hydrogen, which for our disgrace is sinisterly utilized in the hydrogen bomb, is by all means something absolutely insufficient in order to impel the planet Earth to great distances.

Nevertheless, in accordance with this already cited man of science, such an ominous problem could be resolved by utilizing the nuclear reaction that takes place within the sun, namely: to combine four nuclei of hydrogen in order to form one nucleus of helium. This scientific process could permit the technical use of nuclei that indeed, without any doubt, are very abundant in all of the seas.

Froman insinuated that a quarter of this marvellous, combustible material could be used in order to escape from the potent solar gravity.

The mentioned sage supposed that with another quarter of this combustible material, the "all-knowing luminaries" could aim this disgraceful and suffering world towards another solar system and that with the other half of it we could have turbojet propulsion of an interstellar type, as well as light and heat during the trajectory.

This scientific procedure suggested by Froman in order to propel this earth of bitterness could continue to function for 8000 millions of years, time that is more than enough to abandon this solar system of Ors and arrive to other solar systems situated some 1,300 light years away.

Froman stated:

> "To some of us, the most comfortable and unimaginable spaceship would be the very planet Earth. Therefore, if its present position does not satisfy us, whether for this or that motive, then, let us transport ourselves to another place with the whole of the Earth. In this way, we would not worry ourselves with the usual problems of space voyages. For instance: the problem of radiation would disappear thanks to the atmosphere and also because we would travel at a slow speed. The tranquillity and comfort of this way of travelling could be shown in the following projector slide."

Some commentators stated that when he finished the former statement, he had the luxury of showing on a screen in front of that auditorium the pleasing scene of some girls playing golf in a very beautiful place.

To play a game of golf? This does not appear evil! Nevertheless, to want to play with worlds, this, indeed, is a joke made in very bad taste.

But, what if the men of science made an immoderate blunder? What if for lack of precaution they altered the normal rotation of the terrestrial globe? Then what? What would be the outcome?

Have you already forgotten about the Atlantean cataclysm? On that occasion, the verticality of the terrestrial axes provoked the submersion of that old continent.

Darol Froman knows nothing about cosmic laws. It is obvious that regarding cosmic laws, he is completely ignorant.

What could the people with three-dimensional psychology know about the Fohats and their laws?

Do the Fohats have established, inviolable laws? Yes, this is indisputable. Yet, do you believe, perhaps, that people like Froman would accept our enunciations in good faith?

It is evident, certain, clear and manifest that each world from the infinite space contains in itself its own Fohat, its own intelligent and conscious pivotal-director.

What does Froman know about the 48 laws? Has he ever studied the 24, 12, or 6 ordinances?

Darol Froman wants, in accordance with his own whim, to violate the cosmic laws of our planetary Fohat. Have you ever heard of anything more ludicrous?

Millions and billions of worlds are produced in each Mahamanvantara (Cosmic Day). Each planetary unity has, as a fact and by its own right, its own omnipresent and omniscient, self conscious Fohat.

Indeed, to try to supplant the Fohat that is contained within the interior of our planetary organism is not a very easy task.

Therefore, if the henchmen of Froman would, indeed, intend to crystallize such a monstrous project, then the only outcome would be a frightful planetary catastrophe.

SHAMBHALA

The entire country of Shambhala is in the Jinn State; here is
where the principal monasteries of the White Lodge exist.
- Samael Aun Weor, *The Major Mysteries*

Chapter 6
The Sacred Order of Tibet

Papus stated in his *Elemental Treatise of Occult Science* that the true Initiates from the East are the ones who are initiated into the secret sanctuaries of Brahmanism. This is because they are the only ones capable of teaching to us the royal key of the Arcanum A.Z.F., thanks to their knowledge of the primeval Atlantean language, "Watan," which is the fundamental root of Sanskrit, Hebrew and Chinese.

The Sacred Order of very ancient Tibet is, indeed, the genuine depository of the royal treasury of Aryavarta.

Ancient archaic traditions, which are lost within the terrifying night of all ages, state that this venerated institution is formed by 201 members. Its major rank is formed by 72 Brahmans.

It is written in the depths of time and with fiery characters that Bhagavan Aklaiva is the great Maha-Rishi, the secret regent of this mysterious order.

By means of the Holy Eight, the sacred sign of infinity, any chela (neophyte) can put himself in contact with this secret organization, with the condition of having upright behavior.

The Holy Eight horizontally traced is without a doubt a living clepsydra.

If the extraordinary formation of this marvellous sign is intimately considered, it then shows, by all means, the continuity of a single trace. The first stroke encloses a double circuit, while the second stroke only encloses one circuit, which deviates itself in the other circuit after having crossed the sign in the very point of its central crossing, in order to be projected towards the outside.

One circuit is closing and the other is opening. Therefore, this key is what is required in order to open all doors and cut all the currents formed by the atomic energy, from the one (current) which we have imagined and deposited within the depth of our consciousness, until the one which is the originator of all currents and that circulates in the same form (Holy Eight) within the vital center of the Ninth Sphere.

Now then, to evade the usual risks of every astral experience and to attain an inner, conscious, and fast astral projection through these methods, is, among others, more than enough cause for the Sacred Order of Tibet to emphasise its motto:

Nothing can resist our power.

In accordance with the former description, the following exercise is advisable:

1. Enter into mental quietude and silence.
2. Vividly imagine the Holy Eight.
3. Profoundly meditate on the Sacred Order of Tibet.
4. Such a sign joins or separates all the rigid elements by the atomic energy, if this sign is traced over the surface of our cardiac plexus with the thumb, middle and index fingers of our right hand.

You must love the Holy Eight, venerate it, and concentrate deeply upon it. Thus, such a number becomes a clear emblem of the Philosophical Mercury, the true incarnation of Hermes, with which the Initiate must work within the Magisterium of Fire.

Meditate on the sacred sign of infinity, the perfect representation of the living nexus, which wisely links the two worlds (Divine and material) that respectively emanate from the waters above and from the waters below, from that space which is produced in the second phase of creation. In the end, these are united as a vehicle, a channel, and a way of expression of one into the other, within the central, interior focus of the individual consciousness.

Concentrate profoundly on this holy symbol, this ineffable eight, the double current of fire and water that is wisely intercrossed in the Ninth Sphere, within the living bowels of the earth.

Remember the noble alchemical figure of Basil Valentine, a resplendent variation of the Caduceus, the very sacred symbol of the Mercury of the Wise, within which the active properties

of the Sulphur are united with the marvellous fecundity of the Salt, in order to wisely perform the mystical connubial of two luminaries in three worlds.

Let there be profundity in your concentration. Meditate on the Sacred Order of Tibet.

Evoke those eight Kabirs or Kabirim [Editor: Cabeiri] of the sign of infinity, those eight brethren, ineffable Semitic divinities whose cult and mysteries were passed afterwards to the Greeks and Romans. Their special center was found in Samothrace.

These holy Gods were considered to be children of Hephaestus or Vulcan and the beautiful daughter of Proteus. Thus, they appear as being born from the sacred fire that is developed and unfolded within the interior of the earth.

Therefore, these eight brethren are the rectors of Nature, the generators of the vital phenomena, the regulators of all the fundamental activities of this planetary organism upon which we live.

Meditate and pray, remain alert and vigilant as the watchman in the time of war, and do not fall into temptation.

May the ineffable and terribly divine Holy Eight submerge as a precious balm within your tormented heart, and may the eight Kabirs guide your steps towards the Sacred Order of Tibet.

I tell you: be integral, uni-total, and receptive. Thus, one given night, it does not matter which one, you will be called to the temple of the Himalaya.

Ask and it shall be granted unto thee.

Knock and it shall be opened unto thee.

Oh, lanoo, tell me: Are you willing to tolerate the ordeals? The old wise men of the East state that seven are the basic, fundamental and indispensable ordeals for the initiatic admittance within the Sacred Order of Tibet.

Of these ordeals, the Master Luxemil already spoke of the last one. Is it perhaps very pleasant to experience the terror of death? Nonetheless, only in such a way can we come to comprehend that the price of the Self-realization of the Being is paid with life itself.

A lugubrious fate suits me, that is: to contemplate an igneous trail of that which was! I was in struggles; I knew the ordeals. As did others, I knocked on the doors of the temple.

The seducing beauty of the oriental temple laid a flash of life into my suffering soul, like the lightning that, as coloring, paints into the weeping cloud the enrapturing rainbow.

The sacred image of the temple, pleasant and radiant, like a wandering star or a fast meteor, was the lightning that opened an ardent furrow of gold in my night.

This ineffable sanctuary of Tibet is the lamp and the torch. It is the breath that creates and the squall that riots. It is the calm of the spirit who recreates and the storm that lashes.

Fathomless mystery, sweet and powerful harmony, severe and grave, God grant me the ability to have thee as a funeral lyric, a bloody honor, a flower of the abyss, grief, and glory of death.

Across this black river of profane existence, beyond the terrible boisterous sounds of its waves, the austere and grave truth gleams as the silence of the stars.

So, I was submitted to unutterable ordeals, inside, in the ancestral patio of the temple behind those sacred walls. How many remembrances...!

Let the evening fold its golden wing into the void! Let those esoteric reminiscences come into my mind for the good of my

This ineffable sanctuary of Tibet is the lamp and the torch...

readers! Let the stars twinkle! Let those nocturnal birds tell me many things in secret!

Thus, within that patio of mysteries, an Adept-Lady (after many, too many, ordeals, which were exceedingly frightful and terrible) sinisterly showed me the bare and horrible bone figure of death: a skeletal skull between two crossed long bones.

Allow me to live a little more... I am working for the sake of this suffering humanity... I will pay everything I owe by sacrificing myself for the great orphan. Have mercy on me.

"If thou wouldst have been prepared, thou wouldst have died before this figure." This was the answer. Then, a terrifying silence pervaded.

I, vile slug from the mud of the earth, standing abreast of one of these solemn, unconquered columns of that sanctuary... Woe is me! Woe! Woe!... Tremendous memories come into my mind... I was inside, within the Sacred Order of Tibet. However, this was nothing new for me, I remembered that in other times,

Dharmakayas

Nirmanakayas   Sambogakayas

First Logos - Father

כתר
Kether
Crown
1

Third Logos - Holy Spirit

Second Logos - Son

בינה
Binah
Intelligence
3

חכמה
Chokmah
Wisdom
2

גבורה
Geburah
Justice
5

חסד
Chesed
Mercy
4

תפארת
Tiphereth
Beauty
6

הוד
Hod
Splendor
8

נצח
Netzach
Victory
7

יסוד
Yesod
Foundation
9

מלכות
Malkuth
Kingdom
10

THE TRIKAYAS AND THE KABBALAH

I had been there, inside that same place, and standing abreast of the same venerated column.

On that patio, around the sacred table, a group of Nirmanakayas were seated... Those ineffable Beings were distilling happiness.

Oh God! What beautiful tunics, vestures of paradise! What divine countenances! It is obvious that among them some Sambogakayas were not missing, who, as it is known, have three more perfections than the Nirmanakayas.

Lords, allow me to speak some words... The reminiscence from other times are coming now into my memory. Long ago, many centuries before, I was standing here, in this very same place and abreast of this same column.

A venerable elder answered me, "If thou wouldst not have been here before, thou wouldst not have knocked again on the doors of this temple."

Then, while withdrawing myself from that column, I advanced some steps, in order to reverently prostrate myself in front of the table of those saints. The elder who had taken the floor in the name of all those elected ones, stood up in order to pronounce against me some just recriminations.

What a majestic countenance! He looked like a living Christ! Many cosmic days and cosmic nights were reflected within his eyes! His sacred beard was a living representation of the universal Word of life and his immaculate hair falling upon his ineffable shoulders reminded me of the Ancient of Days of the Hebraic Kabbalah!

He spoke and said terrible things. He mentioned a woman whom I had known after the submersion of the old Atlantean continent. "Do you remember such a lady?"

"Yes, I do, venerable Master, I do remember her." It is evident that in those ancient times, I had failed because of her.

"Do you remember this other lady?"

"Yes I do, venerable Master, I do remember her." Then, the living remembrance of a Tibetan queen came into my mind.

7th: United States

5th: Germans,
English, French

4th: Greece, Rome

3rd: Persia, Chaldea,
Egypt, Jerusalem

1st: Tibet

2nd: India and China

6th: Latin America

THE SEVEN SUBRACES OF THE FIFTH ROOT RACE

So, long ago, about one million years in the past, in the center of Asia, in the very heart of the Himalayas, on the side of Tibet, a marvellous kingdom existed. The inhabitants of that ancient country were the outcome of an Aryan-Atlantean mixture.

Every esoterist knows very well that the First Subrace from our present Fifth Root Race flourished in the center of Asia.

I lived in that old country and knew its cited queen, that lady whom the Master was reminding me of in a recriminating way. She came to me when I was a priest from the Sacred Order of Tibet. The unhappy one was suffering. Thus, she told me her tragedies.

The monarch, her husband, was in love with another woman, and it is obvious that the disgraced queen had fallen into desperation. I wanted to help her; I did what I could for her, however, I committed many errors.

To assault the privacy of the mind is a crime, thus to deny my own errors would be an absurdity: I used my psychic powers in an evidently negative way and I even committed the error of receiving some money in payment for it. So, the royal treasury paid me a sum of money on account of the expenses of the queen.

Her husband abandoned his concubine. Thus, king and queen were reconciled for the good of the country.

Apparently, I did a good deed; however, let us remember the words of Master Moria.

Crime is also hidden within the rhyme of poetry.

It is clearly comprehensible, by all means, that I fell into absurdity, that I committed stupidities. Thus, for such cause, in spite of being a Twice Born, I was severely punished.

So, the elder was there, reminding me of all these things. It is clear that my moral pain was exceedingly frightful.

"Didst thou become enrolled in the Order of the Jarretera?"

"Yes I did, venerable master, I was enrolled in it." That was my answer. How could I deny it? The sight of him, most sacred elder, was trespassing my heart. It was impossible to hide myself in front of that divinity.

Afterwards, I remembered that ancient personality that I had in ancient Rome. At that time, the mission to establish a strong scenario for the Fourth Subrace from this Fifth Root Race was entrusted to me. Hence, I utilized the human personality of Julius Caesar.

I formed the great Roman Empire; I fought as a lion in the Gaul and the whole world knows that I was assassinated by the traitor Brutus.

I did not have the necessity of enrolling myself into the Order of the Jarretera, since the secret laws of the great Universal Life would have helped me in many ways, without the need of that cited Roman institution.

Therefore, after these recriminations, I felt ashamed of myself, grievous, and with my heart in pain.

An Adept-Lady, disguised with the costume of a ritual executioner, resolutely advanced towards me while holding the sacred whip in her right hand. Immediately I understood that I had to pass through the evangelical flagellation.

So, I walked towards the interior of the temple very slowly... alongside that very ancient patio surrounded by archaic walls.

"Die! Die! Die!," exclaimed the Lady at the time that she, indeed, was flagellating me with that sacred whip.

Yes, this is what I want, to die, to die, to die, so lash me harder. Hence, those whippings, instead of producing in me that frightful pain of torture, were penetrating inside of me as electrical lightning which were benefiting me, because I was feeling in my interior that those entities that constitute the pluralized ego were overthrown to death.

It is written that Horus must defeat and destroy the Red demons of Seth (Satan), so that the soul can resurrect within the heart of Osiris (Christ).

It is evident, certain, inevitable, that after having returned again to the Second Birth, I needed to die within myself, here and now.

This is not the ordinary, common, and current death of the profane and profaners of this life, a death which infuses great terror into vulgar people, a death which terrifies the multitudes who populate the face of the earth.

Indeed, the death which we refer to is the Initiatic Death for the Masters. This type of death is mentioned by Giordano Bruno, who wrote *Coloro Che Filosofano Dirittamente Intendono a Morire*.

The Initiatic Death is the death of Seth, which is the myself, the mind-self that is so worshipped by many sincerely mistaken ones.

Hence, many years of my life have already passed; however, I could never, ever forget this cosmic event that occurred in the heart of the Himalayas.

Presently, I am completely dead. I worked intensely with the help of my sacred serpent. Therefore, the red demons have been defeated.

The struggle was hard, however, I achieved the Initiatic Death. This path is more bitter than bile. Many are called; but, few are chosen.

The path of life is formed with the hoofprints of the horse of death.

I needed to dissolve the ego, yes: to die. Now, I utter this because...

Chapter 7
Meditations

In this world of cosmic manifestation, there is no higher glory than that of becoming one of those crucibles within the created light of the universe, within which the whole enchantment of the soul is condensed as the fire of the ether within the suns.

It is not true that Brahma, the Universal Spirit of Life, is within himself devoid of that splendid unity.

Who cares if the sublime Prometheus, under the terrible flashing that his forehead attracts, bites the mud of the earth in the struggle, if in the end, like Antheus, he always rises heroically after he falls?

To battle, to fight, to suffer, and to liberate oneself in the end, to lose oneself as a diamantine drop within the ocean of the uncreated light, is, indeed, the highest longing. The Gods emerge from the abyss by means of fire, and are lost within the Absolute.

Many things come into my memory in these instants in which I write these lines... On one given night, while in profound, internal meditation, I abandoned this illusory world of Maya. Thus, liberated from the shackles of this bitter existence, I submerged myself into Samadhi within the world of the Spirit.

There is no better pleasure than feeling oneself as a soul detached from the body, the affections, and the mind.

Immense is the ineffable joy of those Diamond Souls who became lost within the great Alaya of the universe.

Hence, inebriated by ecstasy, I entered through the doors of the temple of transparent walls.

So, with the open eye of Dangma, which is that spiritual vision of the Adept or Jivan Mukta, I looked below, towards the profundity. Thus, I saw many beloved relatives in the depth of the abyss of the mind.

Ocean of the cosmic mind, precipice, cliff, profundity which frightens... Unhappy creatures, suffering women, eyes filled with tears, hearts that suffer... Woe!... Do not torment me like this, have mercy on me...

Let your deviation cease. Your eyes give me grief, eyes resembling leaves imbibed with dew.

So, melancholic and strange, those shadows were dilating themselves while assuming mysterious, smoky cloud designs that extinguish tinted flames.

A murmur of confused and vague words, with profound sadness in the soul... Wretched shadows! Vain forms from the world of the mind!

Just as the furious sea that severely lashes the beach with its waves, so from the world of the mind, from the sea of understanding, waves were emerging that uselessly and desperately intended to lash the threshold of the temple of transparent walls.

Litelantes, the Adept-Lady, exclaimed with indignation, "Those women are too bothersome, they are trying to reach up here." Thus, she unsheathed her flaming sword. I did the same thing.

For a moment, our swords were menacingly turning every way, throwing devouring fire everywhere.

So, those vain shadows from the universal mind, terrified, were lost within the frightful abyss of Maya.

In the absence of the body, affections, and the mind, we come to experience in a direct way that which is the truth.

Indeed, those wretched shadows (egos) from Samsara, the earth of bitterness, are a painful compound of thought, feeling, and desire, which when concentrated in this or that direction, are converted, as a fact, into something similar to willpower.

How different are the ineffable Beings. They are living fires, solar creatures, ardent flames.

That profound sadness of the soul, those eyes with the aspect of leaves covered with tears, do not exist within the Lords of the Flame.

Those intelligent fires of the dawn of all creation are saturated with happiness.

Those Beings of gold, those ineffable ones, are not the suffering shadows of the mind, because wisdom, love, and power are shining within them.

They are the mysterious and terribly divine AH-HI, who dwell beyond the mind and beyond those weeping shadows.

In the profound cosmic night, before the heart of this solar system started to palpitate intensely, the universal mind did not exist, because AH-HI did not exist in order to contain it.

Those mysterious and terribly divine AH-HI constitute the Army of the Voice, the Verb, the great Word, the hosts of spiritual Beings who are so different, so distinct from the shadows of the mind who weep.

By all means, it is obvious, palpable, and evident that these joyful Beings, these blessed Flames, emerge in the dawn of life from the bosom of the Absolute in order to give and establish laws within the living laboratory of Nature.

When the Cosmic Day, the great age, ends, then those ineffable ones cease to exist and come into being. They are lost within the inconceivable and inexhaustible joy of the profound Abstract Absolute Space.

Indeed, when the Cosmic Day ends, the mind in itself and all of its vain and illusory shadows cease to exist.

The Gods know very well that within the bosom of the uncreated light the mind is dissolved like a soap bubble.

The existence of the mind is impossible within that which has no name, even though its potentialities permit the prediction of a remote possibility for the future.

In the nightfall of the universe that sparkles within the infinite, the Elohim must break every shackle that in one way or another binds them to existence, thus becoming radically liberated from all that is called mind, willpower, and consciousness.

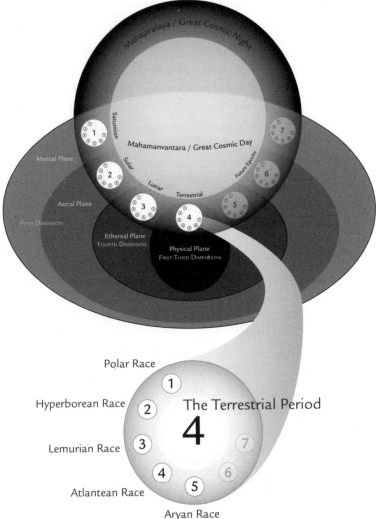

Mahapralaya / Great Cosmic Night

Saturnian

Mahamanvantara / Great Cosmic Day

Solar

Lunar

Terrestrial

Future Epochs

Mental Plane

Astral Plane

Fifth Dimension

Ethereal Plane
Fourth Dimension

Physical Plane
First-Third Dimensions

Polar Race

Hyperborean Race

Lemurian Race

Atlantean Race

Aryan Race

The Terrestrial Period

4

OUR ARYAN RACE IS THE FIFTH RACE OF THIS FOURTH ROUND.

During the Cosmic Day, the living germs
are submitted to the laws of evolution and
devolution, rhythm, vibration, numbers,
measurement, and weight.

Chapter 8
Evolution and Devolution

In ancient times, the great sage Anaximenes of Miletus emphasised the idea that the number of inhabitable worlds is infinite.

Hence, Anaximenes proposed that life, which vibrates and palpitates upon the face of the earth, originated from the oceanic mud or mire, and that later, little by little, with the coming of innumerable centuries, it adapted to the environment.

Anaximenes very seriously thought that all of the living species, including the intellectual animal, mistakenly called human being, are descendants from archaic oceanic creatures.

Epicurus believed in "spontaneous generation" and his ideas intensely resonated in the intellectual environment of the XVII and XVIII centuries. There is no need to mention that Newton and Harvey accepted this theory.

Jan Baptista van Helmont believed that the clue of life exclusively resided in fermentation, and he even gave himself the luxury of proposing methods in order to generate scorpions and other living creatures. The most amusing was his famous recipe to create or generate mice:

> "If one squeezes a dirty shirt through the mouth of a jar that contains some wheat grains, then the fermentation exuded by the dirty shirt, altered by the smell of the wheat grains, will give, at the end of twenty-one days, the transformation of wheat into mice."

Indeed, it is obvious that such a recipe, in its depth, is one hundred percent frightfully ludicrous.

In the year 1765, the intellectual world amidst the lower countries was agitated by tremendous discussions revolving around bacteria and the protozoan. Many believed that such microscopic organisms developed themselves in a natural and spontaneous way. However, Antonie Van Leeuwenhoek suspected that these organisms were originating in the air.

Meanwhile, Georges Luis Leclerc de Buffon, the very famous French naturalist (to whom we owe the much-discussed theory of the collision between the Sun and a comet, with which many have attempted to explain the origin of the solar system of Ors where all of us live) gave a skilful, scientific explanation related with the disquieting theme of spontaneous generation.

He stated that living matter is composed of "organic molecules." During the process of putrefaction, this matter is capable of readjusting itself alone, in order to form new organisms from recently dead matter.

It is evident that the sophism of such an absurd explanation is found based on that "spontaneous readjustment," which is done haphazardly, in other words, without an intelligent, pivotal, directing principle.

Pierre Simon Marquis de Laplace, the author of the so-called nebular theory which states that a solar nebula, or gaseous cloud, was where the Sun and planets were formed (in the origin of the solar system) by condensation, suggested the idea that plants and animals of this world in which we live in owe their existence to the solar rays.

The most intense intellectual conflict of the XIX century had its scenario upon the field of Pasteur and Darwin's ideas.

The very thorny subject related with the inferior forms of life and spontaneous generation instilled violent debates when Charles Darwin made his theory of evolution public.

Louis Pasteur, armrest for the lance, lunged himself against the dogma of evolution when he ridiculed Jules Michelet, who in an absurd way described life as originating within a drop of maritime water, very rich in nitrogen and a little mucosity or fecundating jelly. He stated that possibly, at the end of 10,000 years, it would have evolved to the dignity of an insect, and afterwards, during the period of 100,000 of years, to that of an ape, and a human being.

Louis Pasteur wisely invalidated the theory of spontaneous generation when he stated: "No, presently, we do not know of any circumstance in which we can affirm that microscopic creatures have undergone transformation or putrefaction in such a way, without germs or predecessors similar to them, as to spontaneously generate new organisms within themselves. Therefore, all of those who pretend to contradict this reality are nothing less than toys from illusions, victims of wrongly performed experiments filled with errors which they cannot explain or avoid."

Pasteur showed to the audience who attentively was listening to him a jar containing fermentable matter stored for many years. It is obvious that because such a container was hermetically sealed, the micro-organisms of the air could not penetrate within its interior. Therefore, such matter did not ferment.

Charles Darwin wrote the following in a letter dated prior to the year 1871: "It has been frequently stated that all the necessary conditions for the first generation of an organism are now presently found and could have always been present. Nonetheless, [and behold, indeed, the doubtful reason of his statement], if we can conceive that in a small and warm puddle, with all type of ammoniac and phosphoric acid salts, light, heat, electricity, etc., there was chemically formed a compound of protein ready to even undergo more complex variations, presently such matter would be instantaneously devoured or absorbed. However, this would not have happened before the formation of living creatures."

When Louis Pasteur dissipated into cosmic dust the theory of spontaneous generation, he also annulled the foundation of Charles Darwin's theory of evolution and transformation.

Life in itself, including the lowest and most elemental life, such as bacteria, can only emerge from other life.

The germs of existence sleep during the profound night of the great Pralaya within the bosom of the Abstract Absolute Space, and come into cosmic manifestation when the dawn of the Mahamanvantara is initiated.

During the Cosmic Day, the living germs are submitted to the laws of evolution and devolution, rhythm, vibration, numbers, measurement, and weight.

CORAL POLYP

Each specie has in itself its living prototype, its original germs.

The living germs of the universal life, intelligently suspended in the vital atmosphere of the world in which we live, can be classified.

It is obvious, palpable, and evident that the surrounding environmental medium in each planet of the inalterable infinite is submitted to various modifications.

It is evident that each specific germinal species demands for its manifestation clear and precise vital conditions.

Any germinal elemental specimen can and must evolve and develop during its cycle of particular activity.

It is indubitable and even axiomatic that when the cycle of activity of any model or germinal type is finished, then it devolves and returns towards its original and primeval state.

Example: coral polyps (which presently in their devolution are just simple, devolving micro-organisms) were in the preceding Round, frightful giants armed with terrible tentacles, very similar to those of maritime octopuses.

The enormous antediluvian monsters that in aforetime were desolating cyclopean cities, leaving everywhere their indelible print of terror and death, still exist - even if this seems incredible - in this present century. Presently, they are simple microbes which are suspended in the atmosphere. In a world of the future Mahamanvantara, those germs of life inevitably will be developed.

But, what can we say about this race of intellectual animals, about these three-brained or three-centered bipeds?

Why would this specimen, sample, or beastly reasoning model be an exception to this majestic rule? It is obvious that the germs of this biped mistakenly called human being started their multiple evolving processes from the very dawn of the Mahamanvantara.

Did you ever hear about the Protoplasmic Root Race? Without a doubt, it is shown in complete meridian clarity that this aforesaid gigantic generation, beyond time and distance, was indeed the culmination of a long series of evolving processes, which had their scenario within the superior dimensions of Nature.

It is known that the subsequent generations of human species, descendants from those enormous archaic giants, have regressed since ancient times, devolving towards their primeval germinal state.

Anthropogenesis teaches that any world from the infinite space sooner or later is converted into a scenario for seven human root races.

Luckily, we know that upon this unfortunate world of too much misfortune, we are, precisely, the Fifth Generation.

It is obvious that the Sixth Root Race will be even smaller in stature, and by all means it is evident that the last human generation will be Lilliputians.

In order to demonstrate its realities, nature always has specimens, models, living examples to its disposition.

In the moments in which I write these lines, it comes into my memory the singular case of a certain Lemurian-Lilliputian tribe who, until a short while ago lived in Lipez, Bolivia, South America.

Ancient traditions affirm that the men as well as the women from that mysterious tribe have human bodies that scarcely reach statures that start from 15 to 25 centimeters.

People who live there stated that the curious town where these Lilliputians lived still exists, and that it is situated about 120 kilometres from Potosi, Bolivia, South America.

Frankly, it seems very unfortunate to us that this unusual town, similar to a toy village, has been abandoned by its very small and strange dwellers.

It would not be difficult to guess that such an unusual tribe penetrated into the fourth dimension, in order to transport themselves into another place, less visible to the profane sight of curious people.

Thus, the wise Aztecs were not mistaken when emphasising their idea that "the Children of the Third Sun were converted into birds."

Therefore, in the dusk of this terrestrial life, prior to those moments in which the earth will have converted itself into a new moon, the intellectual animal species will have returned to its germinal state.

It is obvious that after the death of this physical world, the human germs will continue devolving within the superior dimensions of Nature, until returning to their elemental, atomic, original state.

It is written with characters of fire within the great Book of Life, that at the end of the great Cosmic Day, every vital germ must profoundly sleep within the chaos for seven eternities.

Verily, verily, I say unto you that only the music, the Word, the Logos, can awake the vital germs in the dawn of any Mahamanvantara for a new cycle of activity.

OREMUS...

Chapter 9
Egyptian Mummies

Oh, Keb! Genie of the Earth! Powerful Lord of the world, sublime protector of the venerable mummies in the sunny country of Khem...! Hail!

What are my ears listening to? Oh, Gods from Amen-Ra! Still, within the profound depth of all ages, the ineffable Word of Hermes Trismegistus, the thrice great God Ibis of Thoth, is resounding.

A lethargy of eternity weighs upon the very ancient mysteries of the Sphinx of the desert, and the souls of Amente yearn for a new Neptunian-Amentian manifestation.

An Egyptian reincarnation comes into my memory in these moments. Indeed, I was born and lived in Egypt during the dynasty of the Pharaoh Kephren.

Even if my words do seem enigmatic and strange, indeed, I tell you that my physical body did not die. Nonetheless, it went into the sepulchre.

Catalepsy? Yes! Of what type? This is impossible to explain to you, because you will not understand it now.

Ah! But my case, certainly, was not an exception. Many other Hierophants went into the sepulchre in a cataleptic state.

These very special type of mummies continue to live, and without any nourishment. However, they are with all of their natural faculties in suspension. This is something that in no way should surprise us.

Remember the toads during winter, buried within the mud. Like cadavers, they lie down without taking nourishment of any type. Nevertheless, in spring, they return alive.

Editor's Note: In October 2006, a Japanese man, Mitsutaka Uchikoshi, was believed to have been in a near-hibernation-like state for three weeks. He had fallen asleep on a snowy mountain and claimed he had only woken up after being discovered 23 days later; doctors who treated him believed his temperature had fallen to 22 °C (71 °F) during that period. (Quoted from Wikipedia)

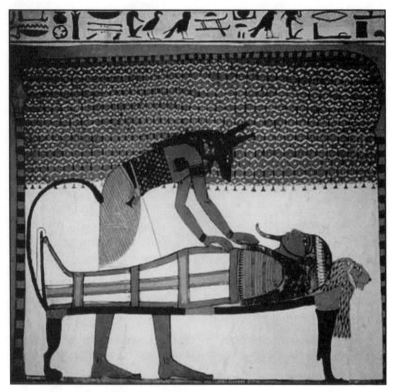

ANUBIS, THE GOD OF KARMA AND THE DEAD, PREPARES A MUMMY IN ACCORDANCE WITH THE LAW.

Have you ever heard about hibernation? The scientific branch related to this is very advanced in Paris. A doctor friend of mine informed me that this type of science is also going to be established in Mexico.

Any human organism inside these chambers of hibernation, below zero degrees, profoundly sleeps. It seems to be a cadaver; yet, it remains with all of its human faculties in suspension.

It has been stated unto us that the first person who served as a guinea pig for such an experiment remained in this state for a whole century. It is stated that such a person is still alive.

Nevertheless, Egyptian catalepsy goes far beyond. Moreover, this type of catalepsy is wisely combined with magic and occult chemistry.

It is obvious that my soul escaped from that mummified body. It is unquestionable that this very special type of mummification was not an obstacle in order to continue with my cycle of reincarnations.

The soul of any Egyptian Hierophant has four bodies:

1. The Mummy
2. The Ka (Astral Body)
3. The Ba (Mental Body)
4. The Ku (Causal Body)

I withdrew away from my mummy, or better if we say, my Soul emancipated itself from that mummified body.

Thus, my soul dressed with its superior vehicles continued to exist within the Amente. Afterwards, it continued reincarnating itself in distinct places of the world.

Nonetheless, a magnetic, sympathetic thread still exists, which in a certain way keeps a particular relationship between my soul and such a mummy.

Sometimes my Spirit enters inside of such an apparently dead body. Then, it is obvious that momentarily such a vehicle abandons its cataleptic state.

My present human personality is not an obstacle in order to perform these type of experiments. No one can hinder the Spirit.

He, my Spirit, can take such a mummy from within its sepulchre, by submerging it within the fourth dimension.

He, my Spirit, can abandon the fourth dimension and enter into this world of three dimensions in order to visit somebody else.

He, my Spirit, knows the region of channels and of the currents, the humid place, the antechamber of this chemical region in which we live in.

He knows how to open the door of Keb, which gives access to the region of the air. He has power in order to call the magical beings, who with their assistance can penetrate into the region of the five senses, in order to become visible and tangible in front of somebody else.

After such experiments, my Spirit can make this mummy return into its sarcophagus.

After my physical death, my soul can definitely reincorporate itself within such a mummy, if this is what TUM wants.

In that case, such a body will definitely abandon its cataleptic state, and my soul, dressed with such flesh, could live as any person, travelling from one country to another.

Such a mummy would again eat, drink, and live under the light of the sun, etc., because it would definitely be withdrawn from within its sepulchre through the fourth dimension.

Chapter 10

The Seven Paths of Happiness

In relation with the Seven Rays of Cosmic Action, there is certainly too much stated and discussed amidst the intricate and confusing labyrinth of pseudo-esoteric and pseudo-occultist theories.

Human machines with viperine tongues pronounce marvellous things! They are people who sleep upon the face of the earth, three-centered or three-brained bipeds who not only ignore, but moreover, they ignore that they ignore.

You, human machines who pass, come, and go... Speak, discuss, if that is what pleases you. Yet, indeed, I tell you that you do not know anything...

Direct mystical experience is urgent in order to know. Yet, indeed, the esoteric experience, the ecstasy, is only for humans with awakened consciousness.

Do you want to stop being machines? All right, I congratulate you; however, you must start by awakening.

Ah...! If the people would awaken, if they would stop being machines... How different life would be.

It seems incredible, but only with ten percent of awakened consciousness the wars would disappear and peace would reign in this valley of tears.

You, sovereigns and vassals, aristocrats and mendicants, know that your miserable existences are nothing else than a weaving of dreams.

THE SEVEN RAYS, OR HOW THE LIGHT OF THE COSMIC CHRIST IS ORGANIZED IN CREATION: 1) THE MOON, 2) MERCURY, 3) VENUS, 4), THE SUN, 5) MARS, 6) JUPITER, 7) SATURN.

On the unknowable high sea, the boat follows the impulse of a bird in its peril. Where does it go? Not even the navigator from Genoa knows it, since he also sleeps.

Sorrows which cheer and joys which blemish, rejoices which weep and sufferings which sing exist within this tragic consciousness that we carry inside, but the intellectual animal always kills what he most adores.

Consciousness that sleeps, how different you would be if you would awaken. You would know the seven paths of happiness, the light of your love would shine everywhere, the birds would rejoice within the mystery of their forest, the light of the Spirit would shine, and joyfully, the elementals from Nature would sing for you their verses of gold.

On a given night - the date, the day, or the hour does not matter - I was conversing with an Adept of the White Brotherhood within the parallel universe of the fifth dimension. Indeed, our conversation went smoothly, and delectably flowed as a river of gold which slowly flows through the thick jungle under the sun.

Suddenly, under the sublime foliage of the Tree of Life, I addressed him as follows, "Do you have a physical body? Are you awakened?"

It is obvious that his answers left me completely satisfied: "Yes, I am awakened, I have a physical body. However, in these very moments I feel that my consciousness is starting to sleep in degrees, slowly, little by little, in accordance with the attraction exerted by my dense vehicle, towards that which people call the state of vigil."

The most interesting thing was that ineffable moment in which the Adept, while ecstatically floating within the sidereal environment, blessedly joined his two feet, in such a way that the soles of his feet made contact together. Then, it is evident that he fortified himself: his consciousness recovered its lucidity.

It is evident that I imitated his example. The Adept explained this clue when saying, "With this secret, you will resist the magnetic attraction of your dense body. Thus, you will remain outside all the time you want."

It is obvious, palpable, and evident that only Adepts like him, human beings truly conscious and awakened, know what the Seven Paths are.

The Seven Paths of Happiness do not exist during the Cosmic Night. Then, the only One breathes, breathless by itself.

Before the heart of this solar system began to intensely palpitate, the causes of pain did not exist, since there was nobody to produce them. Hence, there was no one to apprehend by them.

The vital germs of existence travel properly
protected by cosmic energy within the
bosom of electrical whirlwinds.

Chapter 11
The Panspermia of Arrhenius

Some predecessors of Darwin believed that the assemblage of species on the genealogical trees was the outcome of the evolution of one species into another.

Such a belief is in its depth an absurd hypothesis, because we have never observed the birth of a new species.

Jean Baptiste de Monet, Chevalier de Lamarck, opined that evolution had occurred by the adaptation of plants and animals to the environment, transmitting their acquired characteristics to the following generation.

Charles Darwin went even further in his expositions, with his dishevelled idea that the new types of species were emerging from occasional variations, due to hazard, or to errors of heredity, which afterwards were eliminated by the survival of the most adapted one.

Mr. Darwin, when conducting a retrospective examination along the path of evolution, said that within the confused past must have existed a simple and common primeval form of life, from where the rest of existences come.

It is very intriguing that question which this cited author was asking to himself: "Where do those original species come from?"

In one of his last letters, which assumedly was the last one that he dictated and signed before his death, he emphatically expressed that the knowledge at that time was so poor that any serious attempt in order to explain the origin of life would be a failure.

So, Mr. Darwin died without discovering the origin of life. He wrote an absurd theory without basis or foundation.

Louis Pasteur was more comprehensive. Let us remember with clarity the stroke which he inflicted upon the absurd idea that life could emerge from inorganic matter.

This great sage stated: "There is a peculiar quality within the chemical substances from the animated substances, which are fundamentally situated apart from the inorganic substances."

The fanatics of spontaneous generation were so rotundly disapproved by Pasteur that, indeed, and even if this seems incredible, only a few henchmen of such a dishevelled theory dared to speculate about the origin of life.

No need to mention that the rest of them preferred to select the concept that some miraculous spark was necessary in order to give life unto the first living being. Others, undoubtedly, the most wise ones, sheltered themselves in the oriental wisdom, which states that life is eternal and only the changeable things are perishable.

The germs of life travel eternally through space from sun to sun, from planet to planet throughout time and distance.

Electrical whirlwinds reach the worlds carrying germs of life within their bosom.

The difficulty which the Panspermia Theory of Arrhenius offered was that the micro-organisms or spores of bacteria (which survived the ebullition within the Fauchet vessels) would possibly be killed by the solar ultraviolet rays, a little while after having rapidly passed through the atmospheric terrestrial protective cap.

The rays with more lethal effect upon the spores are possibly the ones with the interior wave of a longitude of 3000 angstroms.

In accordance with posterior calculations performed by Carl Sagan, in the famous University of Berkeley, California, these spores could not have survived, not even during the trajectory from Earth to Mars, or vice versa.

Notwithstanding, Sagan affirmed that the ultraviolet rays are very weak in those distances from the sun to planets like Uranus and Neptune, and that concerning these mentioned planets, the theory of Panspermia is not discarded at all. Even though, in accordance with Sagan, it is not applicable to the origin of life on the Earth.

We, the Gnostics, go further beyond. We are not speaking of spores. We affirm that the elemental germs of life are taken and brought by electric whirlwinds.

If the elemental germs of universal life were not be carefully protected during their interplanetary voyages, they would be annihilated by the solar ultraviolet rays.

Therefore, the vital germs of existence travel properly protected by cosmic energy within the bosom of electrical whirlwinds.

These elemental germs evolve and are developed wherever they find vital, specific conditions.

Devolving ages come after any evolving cycle. Thus, the species return towards their primeval, germinal state.

The evolution and devolution of each species in particular demands precise vital conditions.

All of the living species which had evolved and devolved on the planet Earth have repeated identical processes on other planets.

The theory of Panspermia of Arrhenius has been perfected by the Gnostics and it is obvious that its basis is exact.

ATHENA

Chapter 12
Egyptian Mysteries

Hail, oh blessed Goddess Athena-Neith! How grand are thy works and marvels!

The Gods and those who are wise know very well that thou art the divine Clytone from the submerged Atlantis.

It is written with fiery characters in the great book of life that thou, oh Goddess, knew how to intelligently select the best of Vulcan's seed in order to found the august city of Athens.

Oh Neith! Thou established Sais on the Nile's delta. The sunny country of Khem reverently bends itself before thee.

Hail...! Hail...! Hail...!

The phrases uttered by the priest of Sais still resound from within the depth of the centuries:

> Alas Solon, Solon, ye Greeks are nothing but children! There is not even an Elder in Greece!

> Ye all are young in your souls, since ye do not treasure any truly ancient opinion which cometh forth from an archaic tradition.

> Ye do not possess, no, indeed, any knowledge whitened through time, and behold, this is why throughout the course of the centuries, the destruction of mankind and of entire countries has occurred in great number. The majority of these destructions has been by fire and by water and the minority by thousands of other diverse causes.

> Thus, this is how, among ye, exists that old tradition which states that in ancient times, Phaeton, the son of the sun, when willing himself to drive his father's chariot, burned the earth and then perished by the lightning that struck him.

> Such a tale is of a fabulous character. However, the truth which such sort of a fable hides under its symbol is that all of the many celestial bodies that move in their orbits suffer perturbations that, in time, determine a periodical destruction of the terrestrial things by a great fire.

THE NILE

In such catastrophes, people who live in the mountains, in elevated and in arid places die faster than those who dwell at the shores of the seas and rivers.

This is why the Nile, to which in many ways we owe our life, saved us then from such a tremendous disaster. Thus, when the Gods submerged the earth in order to purify it, not all the oxherds and shepherds perished over the mountains. At least the inhabitants of your cities were carried little by little out towards the sea by following the stream of the rivers.

Nonetheless, in our country, the rains have never fecundated our fields such as they did with others' fields, not then, nor in any epoch, because nature has determined that the water should come to us from our own land through the river.

This is the cause why our country can preserve the most ancient traditions, because neither the very extreme heats nor the excessive rains have despoiled it from its inhabitants. In addition, if the human race can certainly increase or decrease in number of individuals, it will never reach its complete disappearance from the face of the earth.

Through this way and for this reason, all that has been created as beautiful, great, or memorable in any given aspect, whether in your country or in our country, or any other country, is written - since many centuries ago - and preserved in our temples. However, among us and the rest of the countries,

*the use of writing and of all that which is necessary for a
civilized state does not come from a very recent epoch. Thus,
suddenly, with determined intervals, what falls upon us as a
cruel pestilence are torrents which precipitate themselves from
heaven, which do not allow any subsistence, but only of men
who are strange to the letters and to the muses. Consequently, ye
are recommencing, so to say, your infancy again, thus ye ignore
every event of your country or our country which goes back into
a forgone time.*

*Therefore, Solon, all of those genealogical details which thou
hast given unto us, in relation with thy country, look like mere
infantile tales.*

*Of course, ye speaketh unto us about a deluge, when indeed
many deluges have been formerly verified.*

*Moreover, ye ignore that in your country another more
excellent and perfect race of men existed, who perished with the
exception of a small number, from whom you and the rest of thy
nation descended.*

*Ye do not know it, because the first descendants of that race died
without transmitting anything in writing throughout many
generations. Therefore, Solon, in those times, before the last
great destruction by the waters, this same Republic of Athens,
which then already existed, was admirable in war. It was
distinguished over all because of the prudence and wisdom of its
laws, as well as for its generous actions, and it counted, to that
end, among the most beautiful institutions which have ever been
heard to exist under the heavens.*

Solon added that he became astonished when hearing such
a narration and that filled with infinite curiosity, he begged
unto the Egyptian priests to amplify their narratives.

I was reincarnated in the sacred land of the Pharaohs during
the dynasty of the Pharaoh Kephren.

I knew in depth the ancient mysteries from secret Egypt.
Verily, I say unto you, that I have never forgotten them.

Marvellous events come into my memory in these precise
moments.

On a given evening - it does not matter which one - slowly walking over the sands of the desert under the ardent rays of the tropical sun, I, like a somnambulist, silently passed through a mysterious street with millenarian sphinxes in view of the exotic sight of a nomad tribe who were observing me from their tents.

Thus, at the venerated shadow of a very ancient pyramid, I, approaching it for a while, had to momentarily rest in order to patiently fix the laces of one of my sandals.

Afterwards, diligently, I searched with anxiety for the august entrance. I was longing to return to the straight path.

The Guardian, as always, was at the mysterious threshold. It was impossible to forget that hieratical figure with a bronze countenance and protruding cheekbones.

Such a man was a colossus... He was grasping the terrible sword in his right hand with heroism. His whole countenance was formidable and there is no doubt that he was wearing, by his own right, the Masonic Apron.

The cross-examination was very severe:

QUESTION: "Who art thou?"

ANSWER: "I am a blind supplicant who comes in search of light."

QUESTION: "What dost thou want?"

ANSWER: "Light."

(It would be very long to transcribe here, within the lines of this chapter, the whole verbal exam in question).

Afterwards, in a way that I qualify as violent, I was deprived of every metallic object, even my tunic and sandals.

What is most interesting was the moment in which this Herculean man took me by the hand in order to introduce me inside of the sanctuary. Unforgettable were those moments in which the heavy door spun upon its hinges of steel and produced that mysterious note DO from ancient Egypt.

What happened thereafter - the macabre encounter with the "terrible Brother," the ordeals of fire, air, water and earth

- can be found by any illuminated one within the memories of Nature.

I had to control myself as best I could while in the ordeal of fire, since I had to pass through a hall in flames. The floor was filled with steel beams burning with red hot living fire. The path between those rafters of ardent steel was very narrow; scarcely was there space to place the feet. In those times, many aspirants died in this venture.

I still remember with horror that steel metal ring nailed to a rock. In the depths below, only the horrifying precipice was shown tenebrously. Nonetheless, I became victorious in the ordeal of air. There, where others perished, I triumphed.

Many centuries have passed and still I cannot forget, in spite of the dust of too many years, those sacred crocodiles of the lake. If it was not for the magical conjurations, I would have been devoured by those reptiles, which always happened to other aspirants.

Innumerable unhappy ones were crunched and broken asunder by the rocks in the ordeal of earth, but I triumphed. I saw with indifference two boulders which, while closing themselves over me, were menacing my existence, menacing to reduce me into cosmic dust.

Indeed, I am nothing other than a miserable slug from the mud of the earth; yet, I became victorious.

Thus, this is how after having suffered too much, I returned to the path of the revolution of the consciousness.

I was welcomed into the Initiatic College: I was solemnly dressed with the tunic of white linen of the Priests of Isis, and the Egyptian Tau Cross was placed on my chest.

> *Homage to thee, Oh Ra! when thou risest in heaven's horizon as TUM (the Father), and when thou culminate in the heavens as Horus (the Innermost).*

> *Thou art adored by me when thy beauties are before mine eyes and when thy radiant (solar) beams falleth upon my body on earth.*

Thou goest forth to thy setting in thine heavenly boat (the King Star, the Sun), peace then is extended over the extensions of heaven.

Lo and behold that the sails are swollen by the blows of the wind and thine heart swelleth with joy, thus, with a swift soaring it traverses the heavens.

Thou stridest over the heavens in peace and thy foes are cast down. When travelling in their orbits, the Planetary Genii sing hymns of glory unto thee.

The Genii of the stars which never fail prostrate before thee and sing hymns of praise unto thee as thou sinkest to rest in the horizon behind the mountains of the west (because thou art the Solar Logos).

O thou who art beautiful at morn and at eve, Oh thou, Lord of Life and of the Order of the Worlds!

Homage to thee, Oh thou who art Ra, when thou risest on the horizon and when thou as TUM (the Father) settest in beauty at eve!

For indeed, thy (solar) beams are beautiful when thou shinest in thine whole splendour on the highest back of the canopy of heaven!

There is where NUT (thy Divine Mother Kundalini), who brought thee into the world, abideth.

Oh thou who art crowned King of the Gods. The Goddess NUT from the heavenly ocean, thy Mother, doeth homage unto thee.

The everlasting and never-changing order, the equilibrium of the worlds embraceth thee at morn when thou risest until the eve when thou settest. Thou stridest abroad over the heavens in thy journey (thou art the Christ-Sun).

Thine heart rejoiceth and the heavenly lake is appeased. The Demon (the Ego, the pluralized "I") hath fallen to the ground! His arms and his hands have been hacked off, and the knife hath severed the joints, the vertebrae of his body (this is what happens when we dissolve the ego).

Ra hath a fair wind, his heavenly boat goeth forth and sailing along, bloweth by propitious winds it cometh into port. The

Divinities of the south and of the north, of the west and of the east praise thee, Oh thou, Divine Substance, from whom all forms of life come into Being...!

Lo and behold, thou sendest forth the word, and the earth listens flooded with silence..!

Oh thou, Unique Divinity, (Solar Christ), who didst reign in heaven before ever the earth and the mountains came into existence...

O Runner! Oh thou, the Lord! Thou, the Unique One! Thou, the Creator of all that existeth!

In thy rising at the Dawn of ancient times, Thou hast fashioned the tongue of the company of the Divine Hierarchies (He places the word in the larynx of the Gods).

Thou hast ploughed up the beings and whatsoever cometh forth from the First Ocean (the Chaos) and thou hast sheltereth them over the flooded land of the lake of HORUS (the Innermost)...

Let me snuff the air which cometh forth from thy nostrils and the North Wind which cometh forth from thy Mother Nut (the Divine Mother Kundalini)!

Oh Ra! make thou to be sanctified my shining form, my spirit! Oh Osiris! restore thou the divine nature of my soul! Glory unto thee, Oh Lord of Gods! May thy name be glorified.

Oh thou, creator of wondrous works, shine thou with thy rays of light upon my body which reposes on the earth for all eternity.

(This is a textual prayer taken from *The Egyptian Book of the Occult Abode*).

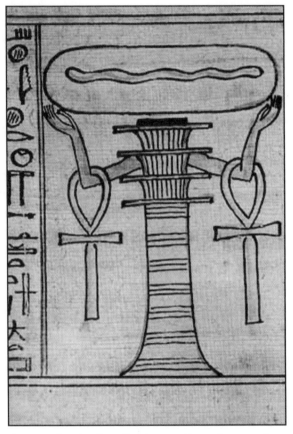

A SYMBOL OF OSIRIS (THE COSMIC CHRIST) FROM THE EGYPTIAN BOOK OF THE DEAD: A DJED-PILLAR (THE SPINAL COLUMN) HOLDS ALOFT A SERPENT.

That which is the mystery, that which we do not understand, is dark for the human intellect.

Chapter 13
Dark Light

"Osiris is a dark God." These terrible, frightful words, this unusual, mysterious phrase, was secretly pronounced in the concealment of the temples, during the Initiatic ceremonies in the sunny country of Khem.

Gods and humans know very well that Osiris Numen, the Egyptian God, deep in thought, is absolutely incomprehensible to us all.

That which is the mystery, that which we do not understand, is dark for the human intellect. Now, after this explanation, our readers can comprehend the deep meaning of that mysterious phrase.

In the beginning or dawn of each universe, the Eternal Dark Light, or Absolute Obscurity is converted into the Chaos.

It is written and with words of fire within all the sacred books of the world that the Chaos is the seed-plot of the Cosmos.

The Nothingness, the Chaos, is certainly and without the least bit of doubt the Alpha and the Omega, the beginning and the end of all the worlds that live and palpitate within the inalterable infinite.

The *Aitareya Brahmana*, a precious and magisterial lesson of the Rig Veda, has truly demonstrated until satiation the tremendous identity between the luminous ideas of Brahmans and Pythagorians, because Brahmans and Pythagorians are supported by mathematics.

In the previously cited Hindustani book, the dark fire, the abstract, obscure Wisdom, the Absolute Light, unconditioned and without name, is frequently mentioned.

The abstract Seity, the primeval Zero-Aster of Parsis, is the life-saturated Nothingness. It is That... That... That...

God himself, in other words, the Army of the Voice, the great Word, dies when the great Pralaya, the Cosmic Night, arrives, and is reborn terribly divine in the dawn of the Mahamanvantara.

The absolutely radical zero in transcendental arithmetics, the abstract space in geometry, the unknowable Seity (do not confuse it with Deity, which is different) is not born, does not die, nor does it reincarnate.

From this unknowable entirety, or radical zero, emanates in the beginning any sidereal universe, Pythagorean Monad, Gnostic Father/Mother, Hindu Purusha-Prakriti, Egyptian Osiris-Isis, dual Protocosmos or Kabbalistic Adam Kadmon, the Theos-Chaos of the Theogony of Hesiod, the Chaldean Ur-Anas or fire and water, Semitic Iod-Heve, Parsi Zeru-Ama, Unique-One, Buddhist Aunadad-Ad, Ruach Elohim or Divine Spirit of the Lord floating upon Genesis' waters of the first instant.

In the profound Night, only Darkness itself filled the boundless all, for Father, Mother, and Son were once more one, and the Son had not awakened yet for the new Wheel and His pilgrimage thereon.

After these words, OREMUS... Let us meditate... Let us worship... Let us now delve into the deepest part of our Being. Thus, while in the absence of the "I," let us search with infinite humbleness.

There... very deep inside... beyond the body, affections, and the mind, let us find the child Horus, the Divine Spirit, our real Being in the arms of his Divine Mother Kundalini, Isis, whose veil no mortal has lifted.

Indeed, Isis is the feminine aspect of Osiris, the Father who is in secret. Osiris in Himself is the masculine phase of Isis. Both are the Iod-Heve, the Jah-Hovah or Jah-ovah of the Hebrews. The Jews from these times of Kali Yuga have intentionally confused Jehovah with Javhe, who, in accordance with Saturnine of Antioch, is the Genie of Evil, the Devil.

Let the Gods listen to me and let the humans understand me. Just as the furious waves emerge with tremendous impetus from within the profound sea in order to rumble upon the sandy beach, so does the igneous serpent of our magical powers, our particular Cosmic Mother, surge from within the infinite bosom of Sarasvati, the Eternal Mother Space, in order to rise and manifest herself within us.

The Lord is even deeper within. Thus, as H.P.B. stated, there are as many Fathers in heaven as humans on the earth. However, all of them are just emanations of Brahma, the Ocean of the Great Life.

Osiris, Isis, and Horus, the three of You, give a sign and come unto us.

Father, Mother, and Son, divine Trimurti, are three ineffable and terribly divine aspects of our authentic Being.

At the dawn of each Mahamanvantara, the Son, the Child Horus, the Divine Spirit of each one of us, must send the best part of himself, which is his Essence, unto this valley of tears with the purpose of Self-realizing.

The battle is terrible; Horus, the Innermost, the particular Spirit of each one of us, must defeat the red devils (the pluralized "I") if, indeed, what he wants is to obtain a Diamond Soul.

Imagine at least for a moment the Androgynous Divine, the Rasit or Brasit, the Gnostic Father-Mother, already endowed with its Diamond Soul. This is how they are, those who have already achieved the Final Liberation.

Nonetheless, not all the Androgynous Divine have a Diamond Soul. Verily, verily, I say unto you, that many flames are without Self-realization.

Indeed, Horus is the vehicle of Iod-Heve, the indispensable instrument for Self-realization.

Osiris and Isis fail when Horus is defeated in the battles fought during his pilgrimage throughout the wheel of samsara (valley of tears).

Yet, when Horus becomes victorious in the battles against the red devils, then the Immortal Triad, endowed with a Diamond Soul, is forever submerged within the ineffable joy of the Abstract Absolute Space.

Chapter 14
Radio Astronomy

Radio astronomy is an Atlantean science that is lost in the profound night of all centuries. This science re-emerged in our day and age, in an apparently very casual way, thanks to the incessant efforts performed by Karl G. Jasnky of the Bell Telephone Laboratories in New Jersey. His assignment was to track down and scientifically identify the various forms of high frequency static interference that, in a very disturbing way, were plaguing the vital transoceanic telephone communications of his corporation.

On August 1931, Jansky started his observations by utilizing a longitudinal wave of 14.6 metres (20,600 kilocycles). Thus, very soon, he achieved in detecting the sources of two types of cosmic static.

The first source of cosmic static was evidently attributed to thunderbolts, which are produced in a terrific way during any storm.

The second source of cosmic static was qualified by the cited sage as very distant storms whose radio-emissions were probably deviated towards the earth by the ionised regions from the polar caps of the atmosphere.

However, something unusual appeared, something peculiar happened: he achieved in detecting what he was not searching for. It was a high pitched whistle sound, whose strange intensity was slowly varying during the day.

Jansky very sincerely informed the "Proceedings of the Institute of Radio Engineers" that the direction of this strange and mysterious whistle sound was going around every twenty-four hours, in all cardinal points of the compass.

He stated, "In the past months of December and January, its (the sound's) direction generally coincided with that of the sun. Yet, its source could not be detected with precision. Then, its direction deviated, and in March, it was preceded approximately one hour in time towards the direction of the sun."

It is evident that Jansky supposed many things, he made up many conjectures in relation with such a strange sound. It is no wonder, since this subject matter was extremely rare. However, he finally arrived at his own conclusions.

He stated, "The radio emissions seem to come from a unique source or from a great number of sources which are disseminated throughout the firmament, beyond the solar system."

It has been established with complete exactitude that the special cosmic center from where such radio emissions come from is found in the direction of the center of the galaxy, and lies in the direction of the constellation Sagittarius.

This does not signify in any way that other waves from other corners of the Milky Way do not reach the Earth.

It is obvious that our galaxy is a living fountain of radio sounds with various zones of great intensity of emission.

The Logos sounds and our Milky Way is not mute. It sustains itself by means of the Word, by means of the sound, by means of the spermatic and luminous Fiat of the first instant.

In the beginning was the Word and the Word was with God and the Word was God.

The sound, the Word, the creator word propagates itself everywhere, it reaches all places.

It is obvious that the exceedingly frightful Second World War impeded every new progress in radio astronomy.

In February 1942, British radar operators denounced a new form of obstruction adopted by the Germans. Yet, when the knowledge of this new interference was given to J. S. Hey from the Army Operational Research Group, it was verified that such a perturbing sound had its origin in a solar spot.

We can affirm, without fear of being mistaken, that radio waves are an amplification of luminous waves of great longitude. The marvellous discovery that some parts of the sky shine in the radio spectral band signifies, as a fact, that something completely new has surged in the firmament.

Indeed, it has been proven in an integral way that the clouds of individual atoms of hydrogen, contrary to that which happens with the pairs of atoms from the gas of hydrogen, emit radio waves of a longitude of twenty-one centimeters.

Van de Hulst, the eminent man of science, very wisely suggested that the clouds of hydrogen dispersed throughout the universe must be dispersing radio-waves of twenty-one centimeters in all directions.

Indeed, the atom of hydrogen consists of one electron and one proton, both describing authentic, real, and magnificent orbits, therefore, harmoniously acting like two fine magnetic wires.

Just as the poles in contiguous magnets are mutually repelled, likewise, the most perfect alienation of these two particles occurs when their magnetic poles are found in opposite directions.

This is why the atom acquires a determined force which allows it to liberate the electron, in such a way that its positive pole remains alienated with the positive pole of the proton. Once this liberation occurs, the atom preserves a slight reserve of energy.

Then, the best finally comes: the electron is liberated and very intelligently emits the energy in a form of a radio-wave. This, in itself, always oscillates with a frequency of 1,420,405,752 times per second (1420 megacycles). This indeed corresponds to a wave of a longitude of twenty-one centimeters.

It is evident that the discovery of emissions of twenty-one centimeters gave a formidable impulse to radio astronomy.

Hence, it is obvious, palpable, and clear that eruptions in the sun determine the temperature on the surface of the moon and in the most close planets; this also reveals the existence of atomic particles trapped and furiously spinning in distant magnetic fields (as is occurring in the turbulent gaseous clouds from the nebula of Cancer, etc.) which have been scientifically registered.

The first great antenna of the National Radio Astronomy Observatory from Western Virginia was planned for waves of longitude of twenty-one centimeters.

Two physicists proposed themselves to search for intelligent signs from other planets.

In these critical moments of our existence, it is evident that other planetary humanities are sending us waveforms related with prime numbers; they await our answer with eagerness.

The presence of interstellar signs is entirely real; yet, if we do not capture them it is because the means to perform such a task is not yet within our reach.

Many intellectuals will deny the profound, practical, and philosophical importance that the registration of interstellar communications would have.

We, the Gnostics, know that a search of particular signs deserves, indeed, a series of considerable super-efforts.

The possibilities of success are difficult to estimate; yet, if we do not investigate, if we do not actualize the intent, those possibilities will be reduced to zero.

Indeed, one hundred stars with a very proper size exist within a distance of fifty light years.

It is obvious that among the seven stars which are about fifteen light years in distance, three of them, namely: Alpha Centauri, Serpentary 70 and Cygni 61, are completely visible from the earth through the marvellous background of the Milky Way. This invites us to think that the emissions of twenty-one centimeters, which have originated far beyond them, would be forty times more intense than those of other regions of the infinite starry space.

Therefore, the emitted signs that have originated close to such stars, on the wave of a longitude already indicated, can only be captured if they are extremely intense.

In order to send messages to planets in the distance of some ten light years, we would need an antenna like the one that is projected by the Navy for Sugar Grove in West Virginia, providing that the receptor antenna is of the same dimensions as the transmitter antenna, and that it utilizes transmitters no more potent than those which are presently utilized on the Earth.

We must comprehend that since long ago, other planetary humanities established channels of communication that some day we must come to know. They continue to wait patiently for the answer from our terrestrial world. This will announce to them that a new society has emerged in order to form part of their intelligent fraternity.

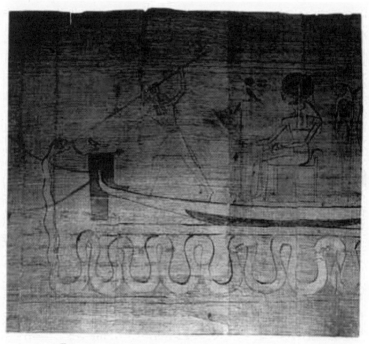

The serpent-demon Apopi (Apophis) attacks the boat of the Sun God.

Chapter 15

The Demon Apopi

After having died [psychologically] within myself, I was confirmed in the Light, and then I entered the temple and signed my documents.

To ascend into the first heaven of a lunar type was the next step. The Adepts taught me how to protect myself against the fatal attraction which the sub-lunar infernos exercise upon oneself.

A branch was given to me in order to smell, which influenced me in a very special way. Such a delicate fragrance had, indeed, a taste of sanctity. "With this perfume you can defend thyself against the lunar attraction," exclaimed the Adept who was instructing me.

Indeed, I know that Adept; he is no other than the Superior Instructor of the temple of the Twice-born. His character is similar to the taste of a lemon; however, he irradiates infinite wisdom and love, without limits or boundaries.

Whosoever wants to ascend must first of all descend: this is the law. Every exaltation is preceded by a humiliation.

It is obvious that to annihilate the lunar bodies was necessary for me, since these bodies were constituted for me like a fatal appendix.

Therefore, I started with the body of desires, the famous Kama Rupa cited by H. P. Blavastsky. Many pseudo-esoterists and pseudo-occultists have confounded such a body with the Astral Body.

It is evident that every Intellectual Animal possesses the Kama Rupa, which, indeed, is the same demon Apopi from the Egyptian mysteries.

Hence, I exclaimed with *The Book of the Occult Abode:*

> *Oh demon Apopi! You must die in the profundity of the lake from heaven, within the lunar atomic infernos, there where my Father who is in secret has commanded death for thee.*

Get thee hence, then, oh malignant demon of desire, before the arrows of my light which inflict severe pain upon thee!

Behold, the Gods who assist me rend apart thy chest without any kind of mercy. The frightfully divine Lion-Head Goddess immobilizes thy limbs; She removes from thee the bestial force that thou possess.

The Scorpion-Head Goddess, the third aspect of my Divine Mother, while walking inside of thyself, transformed into a mysterious scorpion, makes to rain upon thee her cup of destruction.

Hence, Apopi, enemy of Ra (the Logos), disappear definitively. Thou also wanted to enter inside the mysteries of the White Lodge, to victoriously pass through the regions of the internal East while conserving the venom of thy desires. Yet, thou mistook the door, because thy fate is the abyss and death.

Apopi, thou hast been overthrown! Thou certainly hast felt very well the pain that the Scorpion-Head Goddess has inflicted upon thee! The enjoyments of sexual passion no longer will be felt by thee! RA, my Internal God, makes thee, fulminated by the lightning of cosmic justice, to withdraw! He wounds thee! He injures thee to the death! He makes a thousand cuts on your passionate face! He breaks thy bones asunder! He reduces thee into dust!

Delectable enchantments, terribly malignant and fascinating beauties, exist within the sub-lunar, atomic infernos. Remember, beloved reader, that crime is hidden within the miraculous cadences of poetry.

Delectable infernal verses surge from within the exquisite regions of concupiscence, which inebriate and derange. As a mode of illustration, we transcribe the following:

Desires

I would like to surmount that distance,
that fatal abyss which splits us asunder,
and to be inebriated with thy love, with that fragrance,
mystical and pure, that thy being did render.

I would like to be one of the laces
with which thou adornest thy radiant temples,

I would like, in the heaven which thy body embraces,
to drink the glory which in thy lips thou couples.

I would like to be water, so that in my waves,
in my waves thou canst come to bathe,
so that I may, as when I dream alone, with raves,
kiss thee everywhere in a single swathe.

I would like to be linen, so that in thy bed I may rest,
thus, in the shadow, I may shelter thee with ardour,
and tremble with the heaving of thy breast,
and to die while embracing thee with this pleasurable amour.

Oh, I want much more! I want
to hold thee in me, as the cloud holds the thunder,
but not as the clouds that in its billowing rant,
burst and divide asunder.

I would like to blend me in thee,
to blend me in thee to the core,
I would like, in perfume, to convert thee,
to convert thee into perfume and to breathe thee more.

To breathe thee, in one whiff, as an essence,
and to join into my pulses thy pulses,
and to join into my existence thine existence,
and to join into my senses, thy senses.

To snuff thee as one puff from the vault of heaven,
thus, to look at thee calmly upon my life, and prowl
the whole flame of thine ardent body's haven,
which is the whole ether from the blue of thy soul.

The fire of pain is as the flame of the glass within which the myrrh is consumed. Sometimes it purifies, elevates, and embalms, changing the rough aloe that inflames into delicate and heavenly perfume.

I cannot, in any way, deny my intense, abysmal sufferings. It is obvious to comprehend that in the world of the dead, we, the ones who have died in ourselves, must annihilate the lunar bodies.

Apopi, the Theosophical Kama Rupa, is the memory of ancient sexual passions, secret impudence, sometimes mystical and ineffable, romance that deranges, poetry that inebriates with its tales of love.

I relayed myself to the arms of my Mother, so that she could do with me whatever she wanted. Thus, oh God of mine, She saved me.

Apopi has died. What a joy! Now that beast can no longer afflict my painful heart.

The throng of passions has passed. The voice of the ineffable Gods resound on the abutting jungle.

The sexual passion of Apopi has died. Thus, not too far from the nest within which the birds of mystery are cooing with their tender melodies, I feel more happy than the luminous swan who saw from Leda that immortal whiteness.

I am the one who just yesterday uttered the blue verse and the profane song. As the Gongorism of Galatea, indeed, the Marquess Verleniana enchanted me as well. Hence, I was joining to the sublime passion a sensual human hyperesthesia.

Among the living sound of sounding music that animates the choir of inebriated Bacchantes, who drink wine, water roses, and weave dances, I wallowed like the pig within the mud.

Apopi has died. The hour of the supreme triumph, granted to my tears and offerings by the power of my Divine Mother, has arrived.

Chapter 16
The Seven Sublime Beings

Indeed, the Light, the Cosmic Bread, is what nourishes us most substantially. I felt it within the millenarian rocks of the mountain and within the very pure waters of the river.

I beheld it, like a delectable virgin weaving a crown of roses for her own enchanted temples within the imposing silence of noontime.

Ineffably, I felt it penetrating within my soul, followed by a golden procession of dancing atoms.

Down below, next to the timid, singing rivulet, the sacred little herb from the forest was making the iridescent wheels of its delicate stalks to vibrate, and submerged in mystery, a scarab patiently learned to lift the world in each leaf.

Thus, inside, within my anchorite and penitential grotto, in a transcendental mystical experience, I astounded the stones by absorbing the light and imbibing myself in it with infinite thirst.

Indeed, while in those instants, the mundane clamour, with all of its vain passing joys and infinite bitterness, had ceased to exist for me. It had vanished like a dream.

The withered leaves, violently detached from the solitary trees, floating in the air, impelled by the autumn breeze, were lost in the jungle.

The mountain, in the misfortune of its solitude, was exhibiting the mutilated arms of its rocks.

Delectable moments within the silent blue of the profound woodland... enchanted Numen of the shady grove...

The sinner Adam reverently prostrated himself before That which has no name and understood the necessity of dying from moment to moment.

We are not important. Our life has the brief fate of the rose, which lustfully opens in the morning, yet in the night is helplessly reposing.

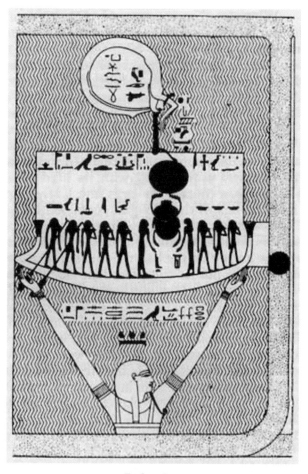

THE SOLAR BOAT

In brief moments the boat of Ra, as a
winged horse which swiftly soars, will set sail
and cut through the eternal waves, carrying
me away from here.

I do not want that sensual delight that corrupts and weakens the wretched intellectual animal.

This world and I do not comprehend each other. My mouth is woeful of singing ineffable things, for the people do not understand me.

The human earthquake has destroyed my heart and all in it expires. The wisdom of death is terribly divine.

Now, there is no bond: everything is broken. The heaven delighted itself like this. Blessed be the bitter chalice that with pleasure I consume. Finally my soul reposes; she lusts for nothing.

Farewell, stubborn world: I will depart very far beyond. In brief moments the boat of Ra, as a winged horse which swiftly soars, will set sail and cut through the eternal waves, carrying me away from here.

Daily meditation is the bread of the wise; it is impossible to reach the Buddha's interior illumination without it.

My concentration was very profound. Thus, while meditating in a more and more intense manner, I finally fell into ecstasy.

The intentions of Mara to remove me from the path were useless; its efforts were in vain.

At the door of mystery, the light of noontime was laughing, and there, in the remote distance, the nubile palm, inebriated with the sun, was romantically oscillating.

On the rosebush from the perfumed orchard of *The One Thousand and One Nights*, the roses were blushing when the crystalline fountain, smiling, was soaping the rocks with foam.

Delectable instants that are indescribable, undefinable, and inexpressible... Samadhi of the ascetic, exquisite fruit of meditation...

Thus, I forgot the body, the affections, and the mind. Indeed, there is no better pleasure than the feeling of oneself as a detached soul.

Then, exquisite experiences, very intimate events, surged within my Spirit.

I very vividly remembered the preceding Mahamanvantara, the twilight of the Gods, and the profound night.

Hence, the moon that in aforetime was a world filled with light and life, decidedly fell on the arms of death.

Then, the Seven Sublime Lords and the Seven Truths ceased to exist and came into *Being*.

That lunar universe was devoured by That which *is* and nonetheless *is not*, in order to be exhaled again later.

Thus, life slept for seven eternities within the profound bosom of the Abstract Absolute Space.

Nonetheless, something remained; not all was lost. Death devours the forms, yet the fragrance of memories continues.

The preceding universe remained, being stored as a simple remembrance within the intelligence of the Holy Gods.

It is written with fiery words that these holy remembrances, when projected upon the eternal screen of the Uncreated Light, constitute the universe of Pleroma.

Garden of delights in the night of the cosmos, infinite enraptures... sublime absorption, inexhaustible joy.

Each virginal spark returned to its own flame. It is obvious that my own was certainly not an exception.

Then, with humility, I studied in the temple those teachings which very ancient Paramarthasattyas (inhabitants of the Absolute) delivered unto us in preceding Cosmic Nights.

Hence, those beings, who now are invisible to all of us, passed beyond our capacities of comprehension.

How long did this ecstasy endure? I do not know; I do not want to know, either. Now, everything has passed. Now, hour after hour, I patiently defoliate the mystery of the days.

Similar to the nocturnal pilgrim, my immortal hope is burning as a blazing fire within the ineffable orchestration of the spheres. Oh, night of redemption, hold thy wings, embroidered with the light of my remembrances.

Chapter 17

A Magnificent Convention

When addressing the truth, it is important to emphatically affirm one's own feeling.

Without desiring to compete in any way with other writers, and excluding very sincerely any vain ostentation (yet, having the risk of tormenting many envious people), it is my duty to confess that I was the first one to announce about the cosmic ships.

During the year 1950, after much dissatisfaction, disappointment, and threatening letters, the first edition of my book entitled *The Perfect Matrimony* came out onto the streets. It is already known that the crowd disputed it and held it as immoral.

Well then, it is known that such a cited book, happily written at that time, clarified the mystery of the UFOs.

So then, I did not evade this very thorny theme. Without preoccupying myself with the reasoning of others, indeed, I very frankly exposed my concept about the cosmic ships.

It is evident that Julio Medina V., the illustrious gentleman with noble intelligence and a generous heart, even after having financed such an edition with his own peculium, also drew these Unknown Flying Objects. It is obvious to comprehend that such notable artistic drawings have true foundations and genuine models.

This eminent Master had the joy of verifying by himself the authentic existence of these furtive extraterrestrial ships. When after a walk along a sandy beach at the shores of the Caribbean sea he silently and quietly returned with his spouse to his home, something unusual happened to him. Indeed, he was surprised by some cosmic ships which, floating in the blue space, were finally lost within the inalterable infinite.

On March the 13th, 1954, the newspaper *The Los Angeles Times* made a stubborn excess of mockery and sarcasm when reporting about a strange convention. It was nothing other than a reunion of people who solemnly affirmed to have travelled in cosmic ships from extraterrestrial origin. This rare event happened in a place in the state of California, in the U.S.A., named the Giant Rock, in the desert, close to the Imperial Valley.

During the convention, a cosmic ship was watched by the whole assembly. Hundreds of people gave testimony to this fact.

This mysterious ship floated over the automobiles as if observing the multitude. Then afterwards, it was lost within the space.

This convention on UFOs was organised under the auspices of the very excellent Sir George Van Tassel. At the opening of the program, Van Tassel frankly accused some jealous terrestrial people of sabotaging the meeting. He said that many barricades were placed on the sandy path that leads toward the Gigantic Rock.

One of the most interesting things was when a very intelligent young man from Detroit, named Richard T. Miller, enthusiastically took the floor. He explained with complete clarity his extraordinary flight of twelve hours inside a cosmic ship of one hundred and fifty feet of diameter, which had been very wisely made up in order to send messages in English by means of powerful infrared rays.

He stated that such a contact was arranged when it was suggested from this interplanetary ship that he present himself on an abandoned golf course, which was situated forty miles from Detroit. Once at such a place, the mysterious extraterrestrial device suddenly appeared, and as soon he went on board, it ascended with great velocity.

Afterwards, the young man described his sensational experiences that endured for twelve hours. He was within the ship by the control deck, where the ship was being manoeuvred by means of gigantic panels.

Filled with infinite emotion, he stated that he was allowed to watch on the screen of a super-television set. It was possible for him to visually penetrate inside an automobile where some of his friends on the earth were trying to communicate with the ship by means of radio signals.

Afterwards, he explained very serenely that he was returned to the golf course by the extraterrestrial captain of that marvellous ship.

Miller and his partner George H. Williams are now working very intensely on what they call "The Telonid Research Center" in Prescott, Arizona. Among other things, it is admirable that he has succeeded in recording on a vinyl disc the voice of a creature who communicated with them from exterior space.

One of the visitors who received major attention from this convention was Dr. Charles Laughed from Chicago. During the month of December in 1953, he received great publicity in all of the U.S.A. when, without any fear, he frankly declared that he received a communication from space, within which many catastrophes for the earth were predicted, together with the re-appearance of the two lost continents Lemuria and Atlantis.

People continued arriving in their automobiles and aeroplanes. Meanwhile, a variegated and painteresque multitude of curious people were gathering around the platform where the speakers were reunited.

Van Tassel started by saying, "We are here in order to reveal these matters and not to hide them. The space ships are driven by intelligences superior to ours. The human beings from space are here in order to help us in this critical moment. We, the speakers, who are united here for the first time, have a duty to do, and we are going to do it."

Truman Bethurum, who wrote a book with the title *The Voice of the Planet Clarion,* stated that he had eleven conversations with people from cosmic space, and he added: "One morning, there were too many space ships over Washington, and the Air Force believed that we were in danger of receiving an attack from another planet."

An interesting moment occurred when the group who stated that they have travelled in space ships were reunited in order to be filmed for a newscast. Next to Miller and Bethurum, there were George Adamski, Dana Howard, and Orfeo Angelucci.

Afterwards, the description of trips throughout the infinite space continued with intensive fervour.

A man who was going around that place with a geiger counter stated that the air of Giant Rock was impregnated with cosmic rays, not knowing whether they were gusts of atomic clouds from Nevada or if they were produced by the spaceships.

Anyhow, the whole world was in expectation in case one cosmic ship would land.

To conclude with this chapter, we state: it is indeed very interesting that this magnificent convention took place, as if in order to corroborate our affirmations, four years after we announced for the first time about the cosmic ships.

Chapter 18

My Return into Tibet

Oh, that time, when a very singular Tibetan Adept-Lady inside the Sacred Order of Tibet said loudly to me, "Die! Die! Die!"

The Egyptian Book of the Occult Abode states:

> *The day when Horus (The Innermost) obtains victory over Seth (the animal ego) and his demons, I am then defunct. I shall triumph over my enemies, during the night of the festival in which the God Djed is elevated to Djedu, in the presence of the Divinities who reside on the paths of Death.*

To die within myself, to dissolve the "I," to reduce it to cosmic dust, indeed, was not an easy task.

However, I have to very sincerely confess that I remained faithful to the secrets of Tum (my Father who is in heaven).

I can never deny that with my Divine Mother Kundalini I entered into the den of Seth (the forty-nine regions of the sub-consciousness).

Whosoever wants to ascend must first of all descend; this is the law. Every exaltation is preceded by a humiliation.

Each psychological defect, internally seen with the eye of Horus, has indeed a satanic, animalistic form.

Comprehension and elimination are radical. It would be impossible to eliminate the Red demons (our defects) without these factors.

To comprehend is the first step, to eliminate is the second one. Many neophytes comprehend; however, they do not eliminate. Verily I say unto you that those ones fail.

The mind is not all. The mind can justify or condemn, hide or excuse; however, it can never eliminate.

This is how I understood it. Therefore, I prayed to my Divine Mother and the outcome was marvellous.

VAJRAVARAHI, A TANTRIC SYMBOL OF THE FIERCE DIVINE MOTHER WHO DESTROYS THE EGO.

Oh, Divine Mother Kundalini! Igneous serpent of our magical powers! Isis, whose veil no mortal has lifted! Sophia! The Gods from the Garden of Hesperides know very well that you can, in fact, eliminate defects.

Thus, between my Mother and I, we undertook the hard work. I comprehended and She eliminated.

An in-depth comprehended defect was immediately eliminated by my Mother. She never abandoned me; She never left me alone.

I learned to combine meditation with prayer. I meditated in order to comprehend. I prayed in order to beseech Her.

Sorrowful, remorseful within my heart, truly repented, I implored, I supplicated to my Mother. I very sincerely beseeched Her to eliminate the psychological defect, which by means of in-depth meditation, had already been comprehended in an integral way.

Then, this esoteric work allowed me to evidence until satiation the plurality of the "I."

Careful clairvoyant observations allowed me to effectively make evident the existing intimate relation between defect and entity.

Thus, I obviously could verify that each error in itself is multifaceted.

It is noticeable and evident for our patient readers to grasp, to conceive the idea, of small, shouting and quarrelsome "I's," which are types of malignant entities that personify defects.

Their disorderly and absurd coexistence inside of our psyche is not an obstacle for these diverse entities.

Unfortunately, these subjective and infernal psychic aggregates continue beyond the sepulchre. The palpable, authentic, and unquestionable return of these abominable and subjective values into new wombs is a mathematical axiom.

Ahamkrita Bhava: These two Sanskrit words signify the egoic condition of our consciousness.

It is obvious that the consciousness, bottled up within all of those entities that constitute the ego, develops and lives in accordance with its own condition.

Atmavidya: With this Hindustanic term we refer to divine Illumination.

It is noticeable that the consciousness inserted within the innumerable "I"s, which constitute the ego, does not enjoy authentic illumination. It is found in a state of somnolence. Thus it sleeps, a victim of the vain illusions of Maya.

Atmashakti: We indicate, we refer, with this term of ancient wisdom, to the absolute spiritual power.

As a consequence or corollary, we can and must even emphasize the idea that while the consciousness has not been liberated from its egoic condition, it cannot enjoy legitimate spiritual power.

When Mephistopheles (the ego) is reduced to ashes, then the consciousness is liberated and awakens.

Now, conspicuous readers, you can comprehend why it was demanded of me to die. Only by eliminating the ego is how I could return into the Sacred Order of Tibet.

To return into this very old Tibetan Monastery was always my greatest longing. Thus, this is how I, after having suffered a lot, returned into that holy place.

Immaculate summit of delights, secret Tibet: everything in Thee has an ambience of mystery.

Indeed, the eternal Himalayas have an innocent profundity, like a mirror. Perpetual clouds, sober Buddhist convents, monks who pray and meditate while chanting very silently: "**Om mani padme hum**..."

OM MANI PADME HUM

These mystics know about the torment of the now defeated races, which lived and died in the shadow of their colossal mass.

They know about the flights of the eagles and about the rays that sign on them with the signature of fire.

On the sides of their mountains roll the thunder of their tempestuous and powerful south winds, and cosmic signs that have a taste of eternity are immersed within their sepulchral temples.

In accordance with ancient millenarian conducts and customs, I needed somebody who could respond for me, a charitable soul, a godfather who would introduce me into the Order. Thus, thanks to God, it is obvious that I had one!

He (my godfather) paid my right to enter - or better if we say, my right to re-enter - into this venerated Order with esoteric money that the human multitudes ignore.

There are no festivities for those who return. This is how it is written and this is known by those divine and human.

Simple and without any ostentation, I returned and occupied my place inside the Order and continued with the duty that in aforetime I had abandoned when I withdrew from the upright path.

I restarted my labor by performing charity. It was necessary for me to help a poor soul inside the monastery who had knocked on our doors in search of light.

> Ask and it shall be given unto you, knock and it shall be opened unto you.

This is love... The fire of charity performs miracles.

Unfortunately, such a supplicant was extremely asleep. Indeed, I performed enormous efforts in order to awaken this soul, but everything was useless.

It is obvious that this suffering creature had not even started to fight against the red demons of Seth (the ego). Her consciousness was completely bottled up within her "I."

Oh! Old monastery, protected by very ancient walls, how much I love thee!

How can I forget the ineffable patio and that sacred table around which sit the Nirmanakayas of compassion?

How can I forget those working halls and all those multiple and varied ineffable corridors through which all the adepts of the light circulate, come, and go?

But, oh God of mine! Remember, beloved reader, that roses without thorns do not exist. You know this!

How much pain I felt when walking through all of the towns and villages of Tibet!

Everywhere, here, there and further, I could see the Chinese Communist troops that perfidiously had invaded the sacred land of the adepts.

How frightful the profaners are! Behold there, the red soldiers at the doors of the very sacred pagodas, cynically making a mockery of what they do not understand.

Unto the divine Padmasambhava, incarnation of the lotus and protector for all the conscious beings, I supplicate freedom for Tibet.

Unto all the sublime Fathers and Mothers of all Buddhas from the five Orders, I beseech to remove forever the barbarian hordes who have assassinated the saints.

Bhagavan Aklaiva, protector Master of our Sacred Order, help us. Remove from Tibet the brutalizing hordes of Marxism.

Ah! The Tathagata (Buddha) knows very well how much I had to suffer when contemplating the terrible solitude of the valley of Amitabha.

What happened with those religious festivities, which in aforetime were cheering the sublime valley?

Now, only the sanguinary troops of Marxism are seen everywhere. How long will this bitterness continue?

Fortunately, the monastery of the Sacred Order of Tibet is very well-protected inside the fourth dimension.

Chapter 19

The Karma of the Holy Gods

Oh, divine Mother Kundalini! Igneous serpent of our magical powers! I suffer too much and Thou knowest it. Even if I want to conceal my pain within the shadows of the forest, it publicly flourishes under the light of the sun.

I love Thee, adorable Mother, as the one who in our fertile, perfumed land loves the wandering bird that in the jungle has its haven. This sacred love that the immortal soul encloses sings with the lyre of Orpheus and weeps within my soul.

I love Thee, Queen of mine, profound Mother, Cibeles, Rhea, Tonantzin. I adore Thee with that sublime fever incited by kisses given without taint, which conceals Thy footprints that come down in torrents of living roses, drawn with stars.

Mother of mine, immaculate Virgin, I feel I am all Thine. What is that, which within my Being does not belong to Thee, from my weak heart of man until my holy and utmost idea?

I live to adore Thee, sublime Lady. My existence, already despoiled from illusions, my incessant ecstasies search within the sanctuary of Thine innocence for the glory and warmth of Thy delights.

Slave of Thy magical beauty, always superhuman, I render my heart unto Thy tenderness.

Speak unto me as Thou speakest unto me....! Let Thine unmistakable accent gladly penetrate within my anchorite ears.

Look at me as Thou lookest at me... with that infinite sweetness of Thy beautiful eyes, beyond the vain illusions of the world!

Profound and good Mother, with pomegranate lips and ivory teeth, have mercy on me.

Dearest holy Mother, beautiful, beloved head with long golden curls of hair that roll over Thine heavenly shoulders, have pity on me.

I adore Thee, my Light, Thou knowest it well. My thoughts soar throughout the heaven, encircling Thy rostrum like the birds which adorn the rich architrave of a temple of hope and alleviation.

I never found in the ages a place so delightful as the garden of my Mother. Abiding there, I forget my worries, I hear songs of birds sweet and modulated.

As soon as I lay down on that soil, I feel myself emancipated from all suffering. I forget every sorrow, every past grief. Whosoever would abide there would be blissful.

The prairie of which I speak to you about has another goodness. Neither by heat nor by cold does it lose its loveliness. It is always green in its whole entirety, without any storm withering its greenness.

The men and birds that yonder advance are carrying from the flowers all the ones which they preferred. Yet, desolation on the prairie they never make, since, for every flower they obtain, three or four are springing forth.

Ah..! If these wretched people would return into the orchard of Eden... If repented, they would return into the spiritual Garden of their Divine Mother: then they would comprehend how vain is their desire for existing in this valley of tears.

In accordance with the esoteric teachings, the real cause of that desire for conscious life remains forever hidden and its first emanations are the most profound abstractions.

Joy of the silence, resonance of the swift murmur, moon of midday, vegetal topaz, sombre jewel, form of that recondite hope:show me the cause, the secret root of existence.

When, of disillusions, thy soul shall become an empire, when thy tears shall be exhausted by thy suffering, when merciless unto thee the world shall apply its cautery, thus lashing thee with its pain, then, thou shalt evade the tempting door, the white door, Tule, the hindmost.

Then thou shalt slowly discourse throughout the garden of thy soul. There, thy Divine Mother in much secrecy shall teach thee the Karma of the Gods, root of worlds, origin of any existence.

Let us wait, let us suffer, do not ever hurl against the invisible our refutation as a threat. Sad, wretched creature, thou shalt see, thou shalt see! Thy Mother is approaching... From her blessed lips thou shalt hear the cosmic secret.

When the heart of this solar system began to palpitate after the profound night of the great Pralaya, thereupon the Gods from the dawn began to weep.

Remember, son of mine, that the Gods also err. Those divine Elohim wrote their erratum on the cosmic page of the past day.

Wouldst thou comprehend now the motive, the real cause of the universe, the vital secret of the conscious life, the desire for life?

When the dawn was dawning, I saw the Causal Logos moving upon the face of the waters.

"Do not begin the dawn of the Mahamanvantara yet!" cried the Holy Gods amidst their sobs.

Useless was their begging, vain their lament. Occasionally, the great Being stopped for a while in order to read the Karma from those resplendent children of the dawn.

These poor children prayed, they cried a lot, as did their Mother with fervour. Hence, everything remained in silence. Then, amidst the quenched sobs of the waves, only the rumour of existence was heard.

Oh, Mother of mine, may thy grandeur dispose of me at its pleasure! Now, for too many intricate reasons, I am going to transcribe a beautiful poem of Don Ramon del Valle Inclan.

> Karma
> I want to build a house
> to attain sense of my life.
> I want my soul to be roused,
> to erect it on stone, beyond strife.
>
> I want to shape my hermitage
> in the midst of a Latin garden,

from a Grimoire Byzantine age,
an Horatian Latin garden.

I want my honest baronage
to transmit unto my son,
so that, through this wand of lineage,
to renew respect unto my grandson.

As a pyramid, my home's harbour
shall be a temple's funerary;

my chlamys is moved by the clamour
of a tertiary.

I want to make my house on a hamlet estate,
and its sunny place must be easterly,
so in its sunny space I can meditate
devotedly.

I want to make my house stoic,
walled with stone from Barbance,
like the house of Seneca, heroic
with temperance.

Thus, let its carving be rocky,
the carve of my house, Karma from my clan,
and let one day to adorn the ivy
upon the dolmen of the valley Inclan.

During the profound cosmic night, the vital causes of existence were destroyed. Then, the Karma of those Divine and human remained in suspension. The invisible which *is* and the visible which *was* remained within the eternal NOT-BEING: the UNIQUE-BEING.

Upon the silvery waves of the warm and transparent atmosphere of any universe that agonizes, as a wrecked and sorrowful Ophelia, the tender serenade of life goes floating by.

Afterwards, the worlds are dissolved. The night of the Great Pralaya arrives. The soul is thrilled with joy. It is the spark that returns into the flame of the Being, which indeed to our vain reasoning is NON-BEING.

Chapter 20

The Beautiful Selene

The latest alarming news stresses the idea that "Tyrians" as well as "Trojans" shall opportunely settle upon the moon.

A certain very intelligent writer stated, "When the human being arrives to the moon, he must dispossess himself of countries and flags, of destructive weapons and imperialistic ambitions. Instead, he will carry the conscience of his own 'humanity' and his best scientific devices in order to investigate the truth about that which might be inside the 'circles', seas and elevated mountains of Selene. This would be with the aim of providing the Earth with metals and resources in general, which could be extracted from the lunar surface. It would be iniquitous and criminal to exploit such resources for war purposes, to valorise 'the rights of conquest' and to pretend that the occupation of the lunar surface is only for one or two countries, thus establishing small Americas or small Russias. We must not carry to the moon our pretentious racial prejudices, neither the predomination of strong nations over weak ones. And if Selenite colonies are established, these would not be slave prisons nor penitentiaries, but communities where co-operation, fraternity and mutual sacrifice would be the condition for a precarious survival that may be painful in its beginnings."

Beautiful words, magnificent intentions, sublime vows! Unfortunately, the crude reality of life is different: such phrases are suitable for Angels, but we are perverse demons.

May God bless the sublime longings of that author! We would certainly like for all people to think like him! Yet, to our disgrace, the reality is very different.

The evilness of this subject matter starts precisely with the "Tower of Babel," in other words, with the absurd system of cosmic rockets, which is the vital outcome of ignorance.

Extraterrestrial ships led by a crew from other worlds should be the solution. However, this demands a major effort and it is obvious that the terrestrial people mortally hate the upright path.

To reduce the psychological "I" to dust, to receive merits, to eliminate wars, to abolish frontiers, etc., is an abomination for the evil ones. Nevertheless, it is obvious that these are the fundamental conditions for cosmic navigation.

Any given planetary humanity who accomplishes with these requisites receives the cosmic ships (the Flying Saucers).

The system of rockets is a violation of the Law. Very ancient traditions state that the Atlanteans (Titans) wanted to assault the heavens. Therefore, they were fulminated by the terrible lightning of Cosmic Justice.

We, the terrestrial people from this century, are now at the end of a new crossroad. The personal encounter with the "Genii" is inevitable. Such an event could be performed on Selene or Mars. In any case, the facts will speak for themselves alone.

The moment in which we have to listen to rules and regulations will arrive. We are now before the philosophical question of "To be or not to be?"

All prophecies, such as they are written, must be fulfilled in one way or the other: either the Kingdom of Heaven is established on the Earth, or the annihilation of all its inhabitants will be the inevitable outcome.

The choice lies in the human being himself. Nevertheless, the initial responsibility lies upon the shoulders of the spiritual leaders of the whole world.

These present affirmations given in this Christmas message of 1969-1970 would have caused laughter in other times. Nonetheless, now everything is different, for "Tyrians" and "Trojans" shall opportunely settle on the moon.

It is obvious that successively more powerful cosmic rockets will be invented, and that in future decades many people will travel to the moon.

It is unquestionable that the great whore (this present humanity) will export to the moon all of its abominations.

It is obvious, clear, and evident that on our neighborly satellite, the terrestrial people will establish hotels, all type of residences, cabarets, gambling houses, brothels, etc., etc., etc.

The lunar night that endures about fourteen consecutive days will evidently give a marvellous spectacle to the tourists.

The lunar atmosphere, which is emphatically denied by the astronomers, certainly exists, although in a very rarefied form.

Indeed, it is indubitable that the non-existence of a lunar atmosphere similar to our terrestrial one is not an obstacle in order for our neighborly satellite to possess a certain "ionosphere."

It is obvious that the ionospheric lunar field possesses a small density, although it permits the production of certain luminous phenomena of a thermoelectric nature. These alone can explain the apparition of variable spots, as well as places of great luminosity or brightness, which are observable during the nights of the full moon.

The decomposition of electrons and ions into "positrons" and "negatrons" or "anti-positrons" evidently advances us to the intimate knowledge of those marvellous electromagnetic zones with great electrical conductivity.

The very tenuous or fine lunar atmosphere could be artificially improved upon with appropriate scientific methods and procedures.

This celestial body (the moon), which has been a source of fascination for humanity, aroused this first impression from Lovell: "It looks like chalk or sand from a greyish colored beach."

The image of the moon, just as it was picked up by Apollo 8 and sent back to the earth, was described by the North American astronauts as vast, desolated, and impenetrable, something like a gigantic pumice stone.

It is obvious and clear that the moon is a dead world, a cosmic cadaver.

Therefore, that absurd affirmation which states that the moon is a world in the process of birth is frightfully ludicrous.

It is also an absurdity to affirm that the moon is a piece of the Earth hurled into space.

It is evident that in some very remote places from the lunar crust, very sparse residues of vegetal and animal life still exist.

It is unquestionable that under the lunar subsoil, possibilities of water exist in some places.

Eventually, the explorers of the Selenite soil could observe the reality of that bridge mentioned by Keyhoe, whose observation he credited to John J. O'Neill, science editor of the Herald Tribune newspaper. [Editor: See appendix.]

It is evident that such a bridge was installed by intelligent creatures. Therefore, it is not a simple natural phenomenon.

The Moon is the satellite of the Earth, exclusively from the viewpoint of celestial mechanics.

When this matter is considered with a more philosophical viewpoint, we can and must even emphasise the idea that the Earth becomes the satellite of the Moon.

As astonishing as this unusual declaration might appear, the scientific knowledge is not ceasing to confirm it until satiation. The evidence in favor of this fact is found in the tides, in the changing cycles of the many forms of sicknesses which coincide with the lunar phases, in what we can observe within the development of plants, and in the very marked influence within the phenomena of conception and human gestation.

The moon, as any world from the infinite space, was born, it grew, it aged, and died.

The moon was a living planet in the past great Cosmic Day. Hence, it had a very rich mineral, vegetal, animal, and human life.

The moon is the mother of the Earth and incessantly rotates around its daughter (the Earth), as if, indeed, it were a satellite...

Therefore, the moon represents the principal and most important role in the formation of the Earth itself, as well as in the population of it with human beings.

It is indubitable that the mother-moon, when exhaling its last breath, transferred all of its vital powers into its daughter (the Earth).

Therefore, the archaeologists can discover under the lunar subsoil ruins of gigantic cities that existed in a fore time, in the past Mahamanvantara.

It is evident that the moon can be utilized as a cosmic platform for future voyages to other inhabited worlds.

Any Jivanmukta or Mahatma can verify for himself that previous manifestations on the lunar world existed.

It is obvious that the Moon was in other times the abode of the Selenites. It is not difficult to comprehend that seven human Root Races evolved and devolved on the lunar crust.

In accordance with the wise Law of Recurrence, which is always processed in all of the worlds, it is obvious that the first Selenite human Root Race was a generation of giants.

Based on this cited law, we can comprehend without much difficulty that the last families of Selene were lilliputians, extremely small in stature.

The devolving regression of this Selenite humanity until its primeval, elemental, germinal state is unquestionable.

The repose of these elemental germs during the great Pralaya, is, as a fact, an axiom from ancient wisdom.

The Law of the Eternal Return made possible the new development of these elemental germs of life.

The Law of Recurrence is being repeated here on the planet Earth, with the whole evolving and devolving processes of such lunar germs (let us not forget that our world is a child of Selene).

If everything is repeated, then it is indubitable that the whole history of this terrestrial humanity is just a repetition, through time, of the annals from Selene.

In a remote future, this terrestrial humanity will return to its primeval, elemental, germinal state. Then, this Earth will become a new moon.

SELENE, THE MOON

Chapter 21
The Black Boar

Opalescences of enchanted and delectable amber, with hyaline fluctuations of a mysterious mirage...

Dilution of light like ineffable stars through a perfumed foliage...

Blond lines like lace disappear on the ground, drowned by the uncertainties of the atmosphere that draws them with its feminine capricious clouds, upon the sweet flourishing of majolica...

Aquatic transparency of spectral enchantment envelops things with a soft cosmic caress.

In the mystery of the night, the living room is drowned within a penumbra of marshy vagueness...

The columns, the amphorae, the cups indeed resemble enormous lacustrine flowers that sleep upon a milky paleness...

There exists within this environment something that cannot be defined... Presentments of anguish float in the air...

Some withered flowers die upon an alabaster glass...

The light of Selene, pale as death, taciturnly enters through the window, pretending to be a shawl of silver.

The sepulchral silence is profound and painful; it is like a great heart filled with infinite presentiments...

Upon the nocturnal sky, sprinkled with stars that sweetly twinkle, the tinges are slowly fusing...

The last solar rays resemble great red scars, which die behind the enigma of the leaves.

It is a strange hour in which the sapphire sky feels the infinite pain of dying...

The Beings and things are born and then die within the profound bosom of an obsessional dream...

The shadow grows, little by little. It becomes gigantic; it resembles a monster that swallows life...

Profound calmness, freshness of the foliage, nakedness of the flourishing night, defoliation of roses from the dusk, which palely fall upon the silence...

Foggy is the globe of the elusive moon, along with a delectable iridescence of mirages upon the cold paleness of the forest, which is filled with a tenderness impossible to narrate with words.

On this delectable night, I am neither alone nor accompanied. I find myself in plenitude. I open *The Book of the Dead* of the ancient Egyptians. Thus, I scrutinize the mysteries of the Region of Buto (the world of pure Spirit).

I know that region. Yes! Yes! Yes!

Down below, I opportunely left my cadaver, my cadavers, my "I," my "I's," within the submerged mineral kingdom, within the underground world, within the region of Mendes.

Therefore, I am a defunct one; this is why I comprehend *The Book of the Occult Abode.*

I know the three ineffable aspects of the Divine Mother Kundalini, the igneous serpent of our magical powers.

I do not ignore, Lady of mine, that You are the unmanifested Goddess Shutet and that You shine in the fixed stars.

I do not ignore, Queen of mine, that You are the manifested Isis, Goddess of the hunters from the region of Buto. Indeed, You persecute the red demons of Seth (our devil "I"s). You entrap them and eliminate them.

I know, Mother of mine, Your third aspect. Hail, Hekate, Proserpine, Coaticlue, Queen of Hell and Death!

ISIS AS RENNUT, THE SERPENT GODDESS

Do ye know for what reason the city of Pe hath been given unto Horus (the Divine Being within the human being)? I, even I, know it though ye know it not. Behold, Ra (the Solar Logos) gave the city to him (the Being of every human being) in return for the injury to his Eye (the third eye between the middlebrow); for which cause Ra said to Horus, "Let me see what is coming to pass in thine eye," and forthwith he looked thereat. Then, Ra said to Horus, "Look at that black pig (the ego)," and he (the Being, the Innermost) looked, and straightway an injury was done unto his eye, that is to say, a mighty storm [took place therein]. Then said Horus unto Ra, "Verily, my eye seems as if it were an eye upon which Suti [Seth, in pig form] had inflicted a blow (clairvoyance, the sixth sense, destroyed because of the animal passions)."

This black boar (the "I") inspires nothing from Horus (the Being) but repugnance.

Only with the death of this black boar will the Eye of Horus again shine upon the forehead of the human being.

Valley of Samsara, obscure night, marvellous solitude, is where my people await this 1969-1970 Christmas Message...

Profound valley, night of the serpent, while falling in love with your silence, I suffer a lot when remembering that, around there, in the world, many people exist who adore this black boar.

Could perhaps the red demons of Seth reach perfection? The black boar perfecting himself through a "sort of" evolution? My God, what a horror! What ignorance! Poor people!

Satan evolving? What a stupidity! What an absurdity! Mephistopheles perfecting himself? The devil performing mass?

The black boar must die. Horus abhors him. This boar is an abomination for Ra. Indeed, the only fate for Seth and his red demons is death.

How deep were my own reflections on that night of mystery. Thus, the hours passed...!

The dawn began.... Upon the deepest blue of the lake, the vague profile of the clouds feigned snowy fleeces.

Finally, the day began to come into view with an indecisive light, like a caress of the moon over the ash of a newly burned mount for the sowing.

Then, the sun shone as a torch of my word, nuptial candle replete with exquisite perfumes...

It is a radiant morning, where the soar of tender doves are mixed with the fall of the dew that descends upon the earth as an odoriferous balm.

A mysterious melody sounds around the sites that are enveloped by an ineffable light, and scatters itself throughout the vast space, as a delectable fragrance, as the breath of the soul when around the sea.

All of these within diffuse clarity, filled with musical shuddering, seem prepared to listen to the miracle of the word: the Divine annunciation of the Word.

Chapter 22
Mortality and Immortality

Ineffable, mystic rose from the profound valley of the Spirit... Immortal Mother of my heart, hearken unto me!

Light of my eyes, rose of my orchard, east from the horizon of my life, prudent as the Hebraic Abigail and amiable like Ruth, have pity on me!

Blooming houri with a flushed color and blue eyes filled with love, bountiful beauty, Mother of mine...

Delicate and fresh flower from the fertile continent of my soul...

Embalmed jasmine from a fruit-flowering garden of Ionia, a cultivated garden with greenness from Erin, without mist from Caledonia...

I learned how to love because of Thee. Indeed, I am nothing without Thee...

Divine Princess Kundalini, adorable serpent... Thou taught to me the secret of the abyss...

Thus, I descended into the underground world inquiring, investigating, searching. So, without Thee, oh adorable Mother, I could have never discovered the gate of mystery where Dante found these dreadful words written thereon:

> *Through me you pass into the city of woe:*
> *Through me you pass into eternal pain:*
> *Through me among the people lost for aye.*
> *Justice the founder of my fabric moved:*
> *To rear me was the task of Power Divine,*
> *Supremest Wisdom, and primeval Love.*
> *Before me things create were none, save things*
> *Eternal, and eternal I endure.*
> *All hope abandon, ye who enter here.*

I knew the gate for the impassive souls and the way across the Acheron. I navigated the boat of Charon across to the opposite shore.

THE THREE FURIES. ENGRAVING BY GUSTAVE DORÉ.

I passed through the damned portals of the city of Dis. I know the profound gulfs which gird such a desolated land.

Woeful is the one who succumbs before the horrifying horrors of the three furies.

Hence, I saw many fallen colossi devolving within the submerged mineral kingdom.

I saw muses, once with flushed faces, now becoming pale and sinister...

I found the glorious tumult and the Bacchants always assisting in order to adorn with their pardalidas.

I saw the Bacchae withering themselves on the bronzed forehead of the abysmal, lubricious Sileni. Thus, the ivies of flowering thyrsus are dried as shrivelled hay.

The insolent consuls from Rome were disobediently assisting with the burial because their intolerable pride was not yet subdued by the immortal yoke of the gospel.

Behind came the lustful courtesans of Latium, the bohemian and degenerated bards, the learned, hypocritical, and perverse religious crowds and the materialistic swine-like enemies of the Eternal One.

Thus, because of the brilliant flash of the axe swung against them, the wretched mortals by the inexorable Parca (the sublime messenger in transit, whom they cannot see) cannot understand any voice that spiritually speaks to them.

Behold there, the famous empress Semiramis striving to quench the thirst of her lust!

Look... farther yon lays Capaneus, the elder from Crete, writhing in proud scorn. He of the seven Kings was one who girt Thebes with siege. He held and still seems to hold God in disdain.

Continuing in this inexhaustible procession is Nessus, he who for the fair Deianira died and wrought himself revenge for his own fate, as well as Chiron the centaur, the old tutor of Achilles and Pholus, prone to wrath.

Oh...! How many crimes, God of mine! When would I finish counting them? In which book would these ones fit?

Black river of lost humanity, devolving through time, falling backwards, towards the past...

Beloved reader, God grant along the way that a soft aroma of white lilies may pour from your life, so that you may drink the crystalline nectar of the honest pleasure, free from woes.

Do not descend my child, because the descending ladder has seven steps and at the end of it is the cycle of the terrible necessity.

To become beast, plant, and stone again inside the infernal worlds... is indeed more bitter than bile.

THE WHEEL OF EVOLUTION AND DEVOLUTION

Devolution: (Latin) From devolvere: backwards evolution, degeneration. The natural mechanical inclination for all matter and energy in nature to return towards their state of inert uniformity. Related to the Arcanum Ten: Retribution, the Wheel of Samsara. Devolution is the inverse process of evolution. As evolution is the complication of matter or energy, devolution is the slow process of nature to simplify matter or energy by applying forces to it. Through devolution protoplasmic matter and energy descend, degrade and increase in density within the infradimensions of nature to finally reach the center of the earth where these attain their ultimate state of inert uniformity. Devolution transfers the psyche, moral values, consciousness, or psychological responsibilities to inferior degradable organisms (Klipoth) through the surrendering of our psychological values to animal behaviors, especially sexual degeneration.

Remember the cruel Harpies who cast the Trojans out from the Strophades islands. Dante found them tormenting the involuting plants in the Averno, making them bleed with their execrable claws.

I want you to know that within the very core of the earth, where the abominable throne of Dis is found, I have seen fossilised creatures reducing themselves into comic dust.

Horrifying, unforgettable, and Dantesque spectacle... Harlots, whores, frightfully fornicating on their filthy beds, strumpets, courtesans, prostitutes, slowly disintegrating themselves, losing, little by little, their legs, etc...

The Second Death is dreadful and horrifying. The ego and the lunar bodies disintegrate very slowly in the Tartarus. It is a repugnant suffering for the lost souls.

"Just let Medusa come; then we shall turn him into stone." The three furies cry, "We should have punished Theseus' assault."

Opportunely, a while ago, oh God of mine... while in a profound meditation, I saw two lost souls departing from within the Averno after their Second Death... Fortunately, they now neither have ego nor lunar bodies; yet, their sacred tunics were indeed stained by the mud of the earth.

The wretched creatures were weeping while remembering their painful journey through the underground of the terrestrial crust.

By now, these souls live again as playful, happy gnomes under the tender sight of our lord the Sun.

In some future eternity, they will enter again into the elemental paradises of the plants.

In a very remote future, they could have the joy of reincorporating themselves again into an animal organism, in order to fly as eagles or walk within the profound forests of nature, or in order to swim as the fish within the deep abysses of the waters.

It is obvious that after many billions or trillions of years, those souls will re-conquer the human state that in aforetime they lost... And, if disgracefully they again come to fall? Woe! Woe! Woe...! How painful is the cycle of the terrible necessity!

Draw near unto me, you who know the Word filled with grace, majesty and elegance, which as Gongora yesterday was polished by Dario, purified by Icaza and subtilized by Nervo.

Draw near and you will see recondite esoteric flows of profound faith and virile bravery, latent in the rocks, in the air, in the waters, and in the fire!

Woe unto you, intellectual animals who populate the face of the earth! Wretched souls with egoic consciousness, dressed with lunar clothes!

Your implacable quench uselessly plots mad attacks, scorning the heavens. You have yet to conquer immortality. Therefore, the submerged devolution within the Infernal Worlds awaits you.

I am now with my open soul going to narrate to you a mystical and transcendental experience... Please listen to me...

The pleasant night was injuring me with its chaste beauty and with its whole brilliantly incentive principle.

We, a group of Gnostic brethren, while holding our hands, were performing a magical chain on the patio of the house.

We prayed very much, yes! Then, we made an invocation. We called Anael, the Angel of love...

On top of the temperate walls, the limpid foliage, swinging with the breeze, was delectably laughing, and the silvery crowned ripples of the rivulet were shaking out the refreshing gracile of its laugh.

A clear and sweet voice disquieted my senses. Was this a voice of a siren or lullaby from the sea?

"Behold! Behold! Behold...! The Angel Anael is approaching... Yes! Yes!" we all answered.

Our eyes attentively gazed at a flock of white doves who happily soared aloft of our abode...

I still remember that bird of silver and fire (Anael), so pure, so tender, so soft... This one was the guide.

"Anael! Anael! Anael...!" we all exclaimed...

That night was sweet and pleasant, tenuous and fragrant... It had the taste of the roses...

A pause came after so many joyful shouts. We waited... We sighed... Those sublime birds disappeared within the mystery, and then....

Three leisurely, rhythmic knocks solemnly resounded on the door of the house. I, myself, opened it impetuously...

"There they are...! They are the ones...! They have arrived...!" This is what we, all the brethren from that group exclaimed.

We all went out to welcome the group of beautiful, heavenly, and terribly divine children...

They were carrying flowers in their hands. While in their presence, one feels as if one is reviving the infancy. I felt the desire of playing...

We can verify that these very beautiful creatures were dressed with the wedding garment of the soul (the solar bodies).

Inside the soul of these abundantly pure Angels, we do not find anything that in one or another way could be similar to the "I" of psychology. Only the Being shines inside those children.

It is obvious that those holy Gods intensely love this wretched, suffering humanity...

It is obvious that in a remote past these venerable ones worked in the Forge of the Cyclops.

Their glorious bodies make them immortals in all of the departments of the Kingdom...

It is not difficult to guess that they radically eliminated the lunar bodies...

I humbly prostrated myself at the feet of Anael, the Angel of love... I needed to consult him about something... His answer left me completely satisfied.

Many years have passed now, and I still continue meditating... It is impossible to forget all of this...

Now, by researching my old chronicles with the constancy of a clergyman in a cell, I write so that others can read.

We, the brethren of that group, still remember the presence of those ineffable beings, their enchanting voices, their majestic countenance...

The light from the pure Spirit touched our temples. It hit our backs with a resplendence that was truncated into lights and shadows, moving as a dance, with quietude in its sculpture and with the timid violence of the air seeming as clouds, treasures, and joy entwining the head of hair...

As does the prism, the waves of light, very clear and empty, quenched our thirst, while sinking us without voices. A pure fire, within slow resounding whirlwinds...

I return into my solitude... to reflect and meditate...

Whence, whence this manifold creation sprang? Who knows the secret? Who proclaimed it here? The Gods themselves, these divine angelic creatures came later into being...

> Gazing into eternity... Ere the foundations of the earth were laid... Thou wert.
>
> And when the subterranean flame shall burst its prison and devour the frame Thou shalt be still as Thou wert before. And knew no change, when time shall be no more.

Prior to the dawning of the dawn of the Mahamanvantara, the unique form of existence without limits, infinite, and without cause, was extended alone in a dream without fantasies. Thus, life was unconsciously palpitating inside the Abstract Absolute Space, within the whole extension of that omnipresence, which is perceived by the open Eye of Dangma.

God never dies; this is what is stated by the hairy bards crowned with laurels...

We sing unto the nightfall of the Gods... The death of the Eternal One is very relative...

Let us raise our chalice and pray....

When the Cosmic Night arrives, the Army of the Voice submerges itself within the bosom of the profound, absolute

and unconditioned Space... It is obvious that God then ceases
to exist within the Universe...

The Great Voice re-emerges when the aurora of the Great
Day begins to dawn... Then, the Spirit of God is moving upon
the face of the waters...

VISHNU

*In the beginning Elohim created the heaven and the earth. And the earth was
without form, and void; and darkness was upon the face of the deep. And the
Ruach (Spirit) Elohim moved upon the face of the waters.* - Genesis 1:1-2

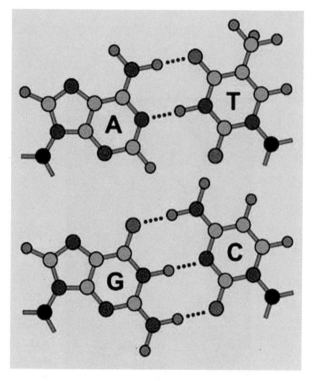

There are only four purines and pyrimidines inside the
DNA: adenine [a], cytosine[c], guanine [g] and thymine [t].

Chapter 23

Constructing Molecules

Rene Dubois stated: "Science's great spectacle still continues with its role; however, now it is represented hidden behind the curtain without an auditorium or connoisseurs. Only the performers intervene. Near the stage's entrance some few loquacious and wrongly informed charlatans sell confused imitations of the great rites to the public. Miracles at a low price have been promised to the world, though they no longer partake of the glorious mysteries."

In the dawning of life, the complex matter of our bodies was found latent within the elemental atomic germs. However, very slowly it developed itself throughout the uncountable centuries.

It is obvious and clear that four basic types of molecules always intervene within the various processes of gradual transformation of organic matter.

Proteins form part of the most important structural matter of all organisms. It is evident that proteins in the form of enzymes concretely serve as specific catalyzers. Without them, the vital chemical reactions would develop very slowly or would absolutely not develop.

Any given molecule of protein has hundreds of amino acids. These amino acids are intelligently linked in a marvellous chain that tends to form a spiral, along with atoms of hydrogen, which, as a very wise nexus, firmly hold these spirals in their position.

It has been told to us that although some eighty amino acids are very well known, only twenty intervene in the elaboration of proteins. In like manner, as the twenty-eight letters of the [Spanish] alphabet can be arranged in order to form infinite combinations, likewise, these amino acids can be arranged to form infinite combinations which clearly express their functions.

Nucleic Acids

The essential quality of life depends upon these admirable substances for the continuity of existence.

The form known as DNA (deoxyribonucleic acid) never leaves the cell's nucleus. It preserves itself as a store or depository of instructions for the correct functioning of the cell.

It is unquestionable that its ally, the RNA (ribonucleic acid) is the transmitter of instructions that come from the DNA's message and are carried to the portions of the cell that elaborate proteins.

The amino acids are very wisely entwined or concatenated during the process in order to satisfy the norm of DNA.

The DNA molecules consist of two spiral chains. These are magisterially ordained in such a way that resemble a double helix spiral staircase of an extended longitude.

The splendid sides of this formidable spiral staircase consist of units of sugar and phosphate. The steps or ascents are linked purines and pyrimidines.

There are only four purines and pyrimidines inside the DNA: adenine, cytosine, guanine and thymine. In a very subtle way, these are indeed in charge of transmitting messages similar to the punctuated and linear code of the Morse alphabet. Those inside the RNA are the same ones with the exception of thymine, which is substituted by uracil.

Lipids

These are a fundamental group of organic greasy matters that store vital energy and form part of the structure of the cell. Their molecules consist of atoms of hydrogen and oxygen linked in a complex assemblage of atoms of carbon.

Polysaccharides

These are a chain of sugar molecules that accumulate energy and that compose the valuable cellular walls in a form of cellulose. It has been stated to us that a cellulose molecule consists of 2000 units of glucose.

Eminent scientists emphasise the idea that the polysaccharides form part of the numerous families of the carbohydrates.

It is indubitable that the four primary elements of these vital substances, namely: hydrogen, carbon, nitrogen, and oxygen, are precisely the most active chemical principles of the universe.

It is worthy to mention the fact, the very interesting fact, that only the proteins and nucleic acids contain hydrogen.

It is notorious that sulphur is found within many proteins, since phosphorus is an indispensable component of nucleic acids.

Back in the year 1930, it was discovered that the atmospheres of the planets Jupiter and Saturn were very rich in methane and ammoniac and subsequently it was verified that methane was very abundant on Uranus and Neptune.

These investigations contributed in order to enforce the idea that the primeval atmosphere of the planet Earth belonged to the methane-ammoniac type.

Indeed, Urey mistakenly supposed that ultraviolet light and electrical discharges could equally liberate molecules within the atmosphere and allow them to cluster in order to form more complex organic compounds.

They searched, they investigated for the synthesis of the organic compounds clue. Miller supposed that the origin of life is found within an archaic atmosphere dominated by hydrogen. Certainly. However, it is unquestionable that hydrogen in itself is the first emanation of the universal primordial matter (Mulaprakriti). However, if we want to know the origin of life we must delve deeply into profoundness.

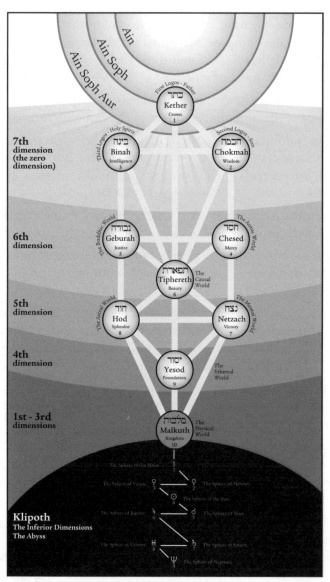

MULTIDIMENSIONALITY AND THE KABBALAH

The word 'matter' is very discussible since it encloses many concepts. The dictionary explains it as: material, stuff, wood, concern, action, thing of affair, cause, occasion, substance, nature, etc.

Therefore, matter is something very intellective, abstract, vague, undefined, since it virtually includes, contains, a whole procession of ideas.

The term 'procession' etymologically signifies theory, when it is used in the learned style or treated in the style of ancient Greece, meaning: theory of the Panathenaea.

Matter in itself as substance, per se, surpasses, transcends, exceeds, the narrow frame of Euclid's three-dimensional geometry.

The infinite processes of matter are multidimensional, this is obvious. Hence, perceiving the things from this angle, it is obvious that the Earth with all of its varieties of phenomena existed before, within the fourth dimension.

Continuing with the inductive system, we can and must even emphasize the idea of an existence even more ancient for our world within that which is called the fifth dimension.

The Jivanmukta, the Adept or authentic Mahatma, by means of the open Eye of Dangma, goes even further: he discovers traces of our world within the sixth and seventh dimensions.

This open Eye is the purely spiritual sight of the Adept. However, it is necessary to clarify that this is not clairvoyance, but rather, it is the faculty of spiritual intuition, through which the direct and true knowledge can be acquired.

The neo-platonic and oriental deductive system, opposite to the Aristotelian inductive system, allows us to comprehend the staggered descent of our world from the unknowable to the knowable, gradually passing through one dimension into another, until crystallizing in its present dense form.

It is obvious that during the planetary descent, all of the vital germs develop themselves by constructing molecules.

It is unquestionable, effective, and real that cells, organs and organisms develop themselves with atoms and molecules.

Inside any given living germ, the cosmic energy operates in three modes, namely: centrifugal, centripetal, and neutral.

If the first of these three forces becomes extroverted and basic for the action, it is obvious that the second one introverts itself, attracting atoms and organizing molecules, while the third one serves as a point of support.

The planet Earth, throughout its staggered descent, finally penetrated into this three-dimensional region, carrying a formidable cargo of germs and organisms.

It is evident for any Mahatma that the most valuable treasure brought by this great ship called Earth was the first human Root Race, who lived on the north polar cap.

It is unquestionable that at that time, the present north and south poles were located on the equatorial zone.

It is evident, positive, and authentic that if we exclude the faculty of intuition, the internal and spiritual Eye of the Adept, then we lamentably fail in these types of investigations, because the first half thousand millions of years related with the whole geological history of the Earth in this region of three dimensions seems buried or lost in a definitive, radical, and absolute way.

The task of re-constructing the mode in which life and its primeval forms might have emerged becomes very difficult indeed, due to the total lack of information regarding fossils from that epoch.

Apart from some vestiges of algae, the most dignified, trustful data dates from about 500 millions of years, that is to say, from an epoch much prior to the era in which the most important events of evolution took place.

"We can affirm with a certain degree of scientific trust, that cellular life, as we know it on the surface of the Earth, exists in millions of other places of the universe.

"Nevertheless, this does not deny the possibility of other types of matter that could be called 'living matters' existing, which in accordance with the pattern that we have formed in relation with our earth might be strange for us...

"Accordingly, we have transferred life from the limited place that a little while ago was considered a special and unique event... into a state of multidimensional, widely expanded matter within the whole universe."

Five are the indispensable basic factors for the transformation of matter into living cells, namely:

1. Formation of the most simple organic compounds.
2. Transformation of these ones into more complex organic compounds.
3. Origin of chemical products, the clue of life, such as the proteins and nucleic acids.
4. Origin of structures and metabolisms (chemical energy).
5. Evolution of metabolism.

Apply the five basic factors of this formula to the organism in process of crystallization and the problem of the origin of life is solved.

Clarification: I am utilizing the term 'crystallization' in a convenient form, so that it can indicate or point to the arrival or entrance of any organism into the three-dimensional region.

It is obvious that the organisms in their way of crystallization were submitted to incessant preterit evolutions within the superior dimensions of Nature.

Therefore, to search for the origin of life exclusively in this three-dimensional region would be an absurdity, an incoherence.

THE WHITE CROWN

Chapter 24

The Revolution of the Consciousness

Fruitful blossoming gardens of solar splendor that burst with delicious fruits are like rivals to honey's sweetness.

Like Orpheus, who tames the fierceness of the brutes with the sound of his lyre, whosoever possesses the attributes of a troubadour shall clarify everything with the Word... Thus, the darkness is dissolved... light is created...

> Lo and behold that I advance towards the abode of the King of Gods (the Father who is in secret).
>
> A winged Spirit leads me. Hail oh thou who soars throughout the expansions of heaven and who illuminates the son of the White Crown (the Son of Man)!
>
> Be granted that my White Crown (which shines on the head of the Saints) could be under thy protection.
>
> Be granted that I can live at thy side (Father of mine)!...
>
> Lo and behold that I have collected and reunited all of the dispersed members of this great God. Now, after having entirely created a heavenly path, I advance throughout this way. - Book of the Occult Abode, C: LXXVI

Ah...! If the people would understand what it is to collect and reunite all of the dispersed members, the distinct fractions of our interior Being, which are unfortunately bottled up within too many subconscious elements...

Ah...! If those wretched mortals would comprehend the necessity of becoming integral, uni-total, complete...

If indeed they would resolve to die from moment to moment... then... indeed! They would radically cease to exist in order to definitively BE.

In the sunny country of Khem, during the dynasty of the Pharaoh Kephren, I comprehended the necessity of returning into the upright path, the necessity of shaping my own heavenly path.

"Whosoever will come after me, let him deny himself, and take up his cross and follow me."
- Mark 8:34

"...Strait is the gate, and narrow is the way, which leadeth unto light, and few there be that find it." - Matthew 7:13

"One man among thousands strives for perfection, among the few who strive for perfection perhaps one is successful, and among the perfect ones a rare one knows me perfectly."
- Bhagavad Gita C:VII:3

"Of a thousand who seek me, one finds me;
of a thousand who find me, one follows me;
of the thousand who follow me, one is mine."

The Gods and those few ones who in the world have become human know very well that the crowds always move themselves inside the circle of the terrible necessity. [Read chapter 22 of this book.]

When recapitulating mysteries in the sacred land of the boisterous Nile, I was able to remember frightful difficulties.

The Path of the Razor's Edge is filled with dangers from within and without.

The Path of the Revolution of the Consciousness severs itself from the ways of the evolution and devolution.

Jesus, the great Kabir, stated, *"Whosoever will come after me, let him deny himself, and take up his cross and follow me."* - Mark 8:34 These are the three factors for the inner revolution.

The dogma of evolution is reactionary. Therefore, let us talk about mystical insurrection.

I, an ancient Tibetan Lama, was initiated into the Egyptian Mysteries after having suffered too much.

Ah! What grief the death of my brother caused me. That was something decisive for me ...

Poor little boat of mine, broken between reefs, without sails, without rhumb, and alone among the waves...!

Fortunately, I was assisted and I studied a lot. I entered into the priesthood college as any neophyte and after successive exaltations I became a hierophant.

That I became both a physician and a priest at one time? This is something that I cannot deny!

I was travelling daily on my camel, carrying a lot of remedies for my patients, a noble Galenic mission...

To forget my haven in that sacred land of Hermes is impossible. It was an ancient, ancestral house surrounded by very old walls.

Litelantes, as always, was my priestess spouse. She does not ignore this; she still remembers.

I have the high honor of having been the educator of the Pharaoh Kephren. I was the preceptor of that young man and I do not regret it, since later on, he became a great sovereign.

I remember terrible things... Those who violated their oath of silence and divulged the Great Arcanum were condemned to the death penalty. They were beheaded, their hearts were wrenched out, and their ashes were cast into the four winds.

The execution was performed on a stony patio surrounded by terrible walls upon which skins of crocodiles and mysterious hieroglyphics were shown.

The unutterable secret is hidden within the Sahaja Maithuna, sex yoga, with its Lingam Yoni and Pudenda.

The Levantine Egyptian light varies in colors of ineffable vigor; it develops infinite powers within each soul.

Spirited light from the hoard of the sacred river, which flows upon the acacia's foliage, is a very sacred symbol of Resurrected Masters.

Light, which is dearest to the fresh rice fields, which perfumes the flower of the lemon tree, is as fertile in festival songs as in the sweet twilight of January.

In the profound night of all ages, the words of the priest of Sais are still resounding:

> "Alas, Solon, Solon, my son! The day will come on which men will laugh at our sacred hieroglyphics. They will say that we, the ancient people, were worshipping idols."

Chapter 25
Alaya and Paramartha

Alaya is the Anima Mundi of Plato, the Super-Soul of Emerson, submitted to incessant periodical changes.

Alaya is in itself eternal and immutable; however, it suffers tremendous changes during the Mahamanvantaric manifestation.

The Yogacharyas from the Mahayana school state that Alaya is the personification of the Illuminating Void.

It is unquestionable that Alaya is the living foundation of the seven cosmos...

When the mind is quiet and in a profound silence, then the soul escapes in order to immerse itself within the great Alaya of the Universe.

Many years ago, during meditation, I experienced this truth. Unfortunately, in that epoch I had not yet dissolved the pluralized "I." Therefore, terror damaged my experience.

I definitively felt myself being lost within the void of the Buddhist annihilation, the infinite ocean of incomprehensible light beyond the body, the affections, and the mind. This was a radical oblivion from myself.

Thus, the consciousness, freed from its egoic condition, was lost as a drop within the sea... That void seemed to become more profound... a frightful abyss...

I ceased to exist... I felt myself becoming worlds, flowers, birds, fish, radiant suns, a humble plant and gigantic tree, an insignificant insect which endures only for a summer afternoon, and a rebel eagle...

That ocean of my Being continued extending itself even more; the non-personification seemed to become more and more profound...!

Not even the memory of my human form remained. I was the whole thing and nothingness at one time.

One step more and what would become of me? Oh, what a terror...! Thus, that ocean of my Being continued to frightfully extend itself...

So then, what about my beloved individuality...? It is obvious that it was also condemned to death...

Suddenly, feeling terror! horror! panic! fear...! I felt myself withdrawing within myself and I lost the ecstasy, I returned as Aladdin's genie back into the bottle!

I entered into time, I remained bottled up within the ego. Wretched Mephistopheles, the unfortunate one was cowardly trembling. This is how Satan is.

It is obvious that the disgraceful one had made me lose my Buddhist Satori, the Samadhi.

Alaya, even being eternal and immutable in its essence, reflects itself within every object of the universe, just as the moon does in the clear and tranquil water.

Let us now talk about Paramartha. The Yogacharyas interpret this Sanskrit term at their own whim. Their opinion is that it depends of many others things (Paratantra). Everybody is free to think as he wishes.

The Madhyamikas emphatically affirm that Paramartha is exclusively limited to Paranishpanna (absolute perfection).

It is unquestionable that the Yogacharyas believe and sustain that in this valley of Samsara only Samvritisatya (relative truth) exists.

It is indubitable that the Madhyamikas teach the existence of Paramarthasatya (absolute truth).

"By no means can a Gnostic Arhat reach Paramartha (absolute knowledge) if previously he does not identify himself with Paranirvana."

It has been very wisely stated to us that Parikalpita and Paratantra are Paramartha's two great enemies.

Parikalpita (Kun tag in the Tibetan language) is the vain error of those who are fascinated in this valley of tears, wretched people with egoic consciousness, unfortunate people who adore their "I."

Paratantra is the phenomenalistic world. Woe to those who do not know how to discover the causes of existence!

A relatively long time ago, while being in profound meditation, I was a witness to something unusual.

Indeed, I saw with mystical astonishment two adepts who, after having achieved a complete identification with Paranirvana, attained the final liberation.

These brethren, attired with their tunics of white linen and their heads covering with a mantle of immaculate whiteness that reached until their feet, entered within the Abstract Absolute Space.

Frankly, since I still have not lost my capacity for astonishment, I felt myself amazed, bewildered. Thus, with wonderment, I accompanied them until the Ring Pass Not (the gate of the universe)...

I saw them penetrate into the Uncreated Light of the Absolute filled with infinite humbleness and veneration.

They passed far beyond the Gods and humans. They became Paramarthasatyas. Nevertheless, they submerged themselves within "That" as simple apprentices...

This is because successive mystical exaltations also exist within the Absolute, which are far beyond any comprehension for us.

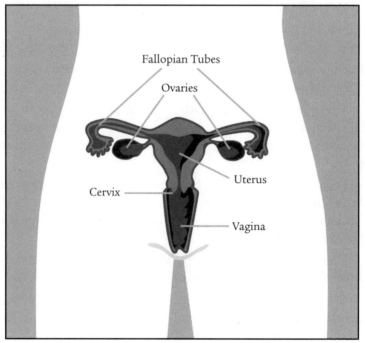

THE FEMALE SEXUAL ORGANS

Chapter 26
Birth Control

The gonads of a female are the ovaries, breasts, and the uterus. The gonads of a male are the testicles, the phallus, and the prostate gland.

In synthesis, such generative glands are marvellous sexual micro-laboratories.

It is unquestionable that the cited glands possess a double function, since they have internal and external secretions.

If, indeed, it is true that the ovaries produce the ovum, then it is no less true that the ovaries also have the incretion of a formidable endocrine substance that vitalizes the woman and makes her feminine.

It is true, effective, and real that the testicles have the Ens Seminis (the entity of semen) as external secretion. The sperm float within the semen; they factually become the vital germs of existence.

The intimate hormonal incretion of the surface of the testicles is the marvellous power that gives energy to the male and is what makes him essentially masculine.

The normal male is the one who has normal masculine gonads. The normal female is the one who has normal feminine gonads.

The ovaries very wisely regulate the distribution of calcium in the woman. This is already proven. Excessive number of pregnancies due to many circumstances originate the terrible cases of osteomalacia or deformities because of softening and curving of the bones. This is very common in those densely populated countries of the world in which we live.

It has been scientifically verified that after several pregnancies, indeed, a progressive loss of the reserves of calcium occurs. Then the bones begin to give away.

Any physician can verify that many women suffer disturbances in their teeth during their pregnancy.

The testicles regulate the calcium in the male's bones, giving strength and stability to them.

Through many years of observation and experience, those who are wise have verified that, as a general rule, the male with very strong bones is sexually very virile.

It is now completely proven by means of profound scientific observations that some of the endocrine glands intelligently act as accelerators for the sexual glands and others decrease such an action.

Eminent biologists of whom we cannot doubt learned that the thymus gland holds the sexual appetite.

It is known that the ovaries emit an ovum every twenty-eight days in accordance with the lunar cycle.

It is evident that such a feminine gamete is collected inside one of the fallopian tubes and is conducted into the uterus, where it has to encounter the masculine germ (sperm), if another life is to begin.

It is demonstrated that there does not exist a more impelling force in its expression like the exertion performed between the masculine and feminine germs when they want to encounter each other.

Birth control is a crime; however, conception control is an obligation.

In these times of worldly crisis and demographic explosion, three absurd systems for control of conception exist, namely:

1. Physical
2. Chemical
3. Biological

Pessaries, membranes, and other intrauterine devices, condoms, etc., are included within the first system.

The second system is comprised of spermicidal pomades with a base of arsenic, mercury, etc. (cellular venom).

Contraceptive pills, fallopian tube ligature or spermatic cord ligature (vasectomy), ovulen 28, anovlar 21, retex, etc., are found included inside the third system.

It is obvious that all these contraceptive physical procedures that are one hundred percent mechanistic, in addition to originating organic destruction that is often unrepairable, also corrupt human ethics in a radical way and conduce towards degeneration.

It is unquestionable that any type of pomades which are applied in the vagina cause chemical irritations and disequilibrium of the cells on the neck of the womb.

It is indubitable that all of the biological contraceptives, the ones which prevent the descent of the ovum into the womb, cause a frightful disequilibrium on the marvellous axle between the hypophysis and the gonads.

It is indispensable to comprehend in depth the tremendous power of those vital agents called lysosomes, because without them the nucleus of the organic cell can never be kept alive.

It is by all means manifest, clear, and positive that the stabilized lysosomes on the spermatozoa and ovum originate healthy and strong creatures.

The contraceptive pills and the rest of the biological and chemical elements destroy the lysosomes from the spermatozoa and ovum. Therefore, this originates sick, insane, paralytic creatures, deaf and mute people, blind children, idiots, homosexuals and lesbians, etc.

The scientists have verified that the pomades which are applied on the neck of the womb with the purpose of blocking it, destroy the cellular lysosomes.

These destroyed lysosomes act freely, annihilating cells and originating ulcers and cancer within the vaginal walls and the neck of the womb.

The lysosomes, in a completely harmonious activity within the living cell, constitute the foundation of existence.

Various forms of lysosomes exist, namely:

Lipase (fats)

Catalase

Oxidase

Peroxidase

Protease (proteins)

Hydrates (hydrogen)

It is obvious that the lysosome in itself is an electro-magnetic enzymatic center.

The k-meson lies within the living nucleus of the cell. When it irradiates towards the periphery, it originates the intracellular lysosomes by means of the law of the eternal Heptaparaparshinock.

The superficial tension, the osmotic and 'encotic' pressure of all the cells (red cells, spermatozoa, etc.) are stabilized when in harmony with the infinite, when in contact with nature.

The detergents, insecticides, spermicidal pomades, drugs, animal hormones, carbon monoxide, etc., destroy the lysosomes from the spermatozoa and ovum, etc.

The vital air, far away from the cities, the Prana from the forests, the sun, the pure water, etc., fortifies and enriches the organism with prodigious lysosomes.

Certainly, the lysosomes are the active agents of the organism's vital depth (the Lingam Sarira).

The physical, chemical, and biological procedures in fashion for birth control destroy the lysosomes. Therefore, they originate frightful sicknesses, they terminate life.

The International Gnostic Movement has revolutionary scientific procedures and methods for conception control.

Our system has formidable advantages, such as not destroying the lysosomes.

Our plan constructs lysosomes, it enriches the human organism, it vitalizes it.

I want to emphatically refer to the Hindu Sahaja Maithuna, the famous Italian Karezza.

Abundant documentation exists about all of this within the famous Hindu *Kama Kalpa* and within the works of all the Medieval Alchemists like Sendivogius, Paracelsus, Nicolas Flamel, Raymond Lully, etc.

It is lamentable that the Hindu *Kama Sutra* was adulterated and deformed in a very monstrous, sinister, and abominable way.

The biologists have evidenced through many years of observation and direct experience that the sexual glands are not closed capsules, since they excrete and increte hormones.

The root of the word *hormone* comes form the Greek language and signifies: anxiety of becoming, strength of becoming.

The astonishing vital power of the sexual hormones is evident. Therefore, to save them, to learn to increte them, to make them return inwardly and upwardly with the sane purpose of enriching life is not a crime.

It has been completely proven that the sexual hormonal incretion intensifies the hormonal production of all the endocrine glands.

The sanguineous torrent conduces sexual hormones, it transports them, puts them in contact with all of those glandular micro-laboratories.

The non-ejaculation of semen (not reaching the orgasm) is radical in order to avoid conception and in order to intensify the hormonal incretion.

If the male avoids the ejaculation of semen and if the woman also avoids the orgasm, then, control of the problem of conception is resolved.

Thelema (willpower) is what is required during the sexual act, in order to withdraw in time, prior to the sexual spasm.

The refrained sexual desire will make the creative energy ascend. This is how we perform the semination of the brain and the cerebration of the semen.

It is obvious that the semen can transform itself into energy. It is unquestionable that the sexual energy rises up towards the brain.

Specific nervous canals for the ascension of the sexual energy exist. Unfortunately, the scalpel cannot find them because these canals belong to the fourth dimension.

I am now concretely referring to the pair of nervous cords known in India with the names of Ida and Pingala.

In the male, Ida starts in the right testicle and Pingala starts in the left one. In the female, they start in the ovaries and are reversed.

These two very fine nervous canals become amiably knotted in the coccygeal bone. Then afterwards, they ascend as two entwined serpents throughout the dorsal spine until the brain.

The continuous ascension of the sexual energy throughout these nervous canals radically transforms us by converting us into mutants (Genii).

We are concretely referring to the Sahaja Maithuna, sex yoga, White Tantrism.

This is the unique healthy system in order to resolve the very grave problem of demographic explosion.

This is the clue in order to control human conception in an intelligent way and without any harm.

It is obvious that for lustful people, non-ejaculation is a frightful sacrifice.

It is opportune to affirm that nature does not perform leaps. Therefore, the apprentice can and must perform this change little by little.

If indeed what we want is the consolidation, the affirming, the fixation of our system, I consider it necessary to start with brief, very short lived sexual practices, as much as five minutes daily.

It is unquestionable that afterwards time can be prolonged in each practice. The great athletes of sex yoga are used to practicing the Sahaja Maithuna for one hour daily.

In no way is it advantageous to start with long sexual practices. This change must be performed in a methodical way and with much patience, without ever dismaying.

The movement of the phallus inside the vagina must be slow and very soft, avoiding violence.

It is convenient to remember that if the sexual movements are performed very strongly, then the outcome is the spasm with the lamentable loss of seminal liqueur.

When the danger of ejaculating comes forth, it can be avoided by means of controlling the breath. In this case, the male will withdraw his phallus very fast from within the vagina and will lie in dorsal decubitus (lying down on his back). Afterwards, he will retain his breath by closing his nostrils with his thumb and index finger.

If he has to inhale again, he can do it, but he should try to hold his breath as much as is possible. In those moments, he must intensely refrain and imagine that his sexual energy ascends throughout the two canals, Ida and Pingala, towards his brain.

The same procedure can and must be utilized by the woman in order to avoid the orgasm and the loss of her sexual feminine liqueur.

In the sacred land of the *Vedas*, any female yogi who knows the Sahaja Maithuna knows how to control the danger of the spasm by means of the retention of her breath.

If while performing this effort the neophyte fails in the beginning, he must not dismay. In the end, with much patience and efforts, he will learn.

After many years of patient learning, the Sahaja Maithuna will become a couple's normal function, the standard of their sexual life.

One among the marvellous advantages of our system is the advantage of preserving sexual potency during the whole life.

In our 1970-1971 Christmas Message, we teach the practical way in order to engender healthy, intelligent, and strong children by will and within a properly planned method.

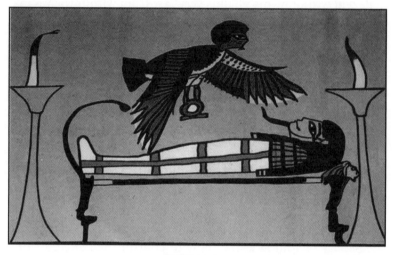

THE EGYPTIAN SAHU

It is indubitable that when the consciousness
awakens, you transform yourselves into
sparrow hawks with a human head. Thus,
you can freely fly throughout starry space.

*God grant me that I might be admitted into the occult secret
and that the contemplation of the mystery of the birth of
divinity be granted unto me.*

Chapter 27
The Egyptian Sahu

Golden clouds bathe the wall. The black crows, still not whitened by the alchemist's work, are cawing on top of their nests, upon which they obviously wish to keep lounging around...

Meanwhile, the bride, the lonely and young soul, bottled up within the ego, melancholically sighs.

Her hands, for awhile, abandon the loom where her fate is incessantly woven and unwoven. Thus, she directs her eyes towards the blue curtain of heaven which isolates her from the world...

Wretched Buddhata, unhappy soul, she is certainly very lonely. Her fiancée... her Eternal Beloved, the Spirit, is journeying in remote lands... All the nights lonely in her bedroom, solitude oppresses her heart and her tears fall as mild rain, fecundating the earth...

The moon is gone and the Pleiades are not shown. It is midnight. Time is slipping away. Meanwhile, lying on her bed she rests... Oh, how lonely she is...!

As the wind from the forest which incrementally shakes the corpulent oaks, so Eros shakes and agitates her, wretched isolated one...

Ah! If she could attire herself with the wedding gown... If she could betroth herself with her Beloved One.

Unfortunately, the wretched one is dressed with lunar rags, with the suit of desire and animal mind...!

If she could know the secret of the Philosophical Stone...! If she could understand it, if she would not reject it...!

Oh ageless stone, so old as the world! Why do people hate you so much?

It is written with golden letters that Hahilla, daughter of Nadir, loves Shebbun, the most intrepid among the warriors. You know this...

The clue, the secret of the Philosophical Stone lies in sex (read the previous chapter of this book).

The soul can elaborate **To Soma Heliakon**, the Wedding Garment, the Egyptian Sahu, only based on incessant sexual transmutations, by working with the Sahaja Maithuna.

Wretched solitary soul, dress yourself with the nuptial attire, betroth yourself with your Beloved One so that you can sit at the table with the guests.

> The kingdom of heaven is like unto a certain king, which made a marriage for his son, and sent forth his servants to call them that were bidden to the wedding and they would not come.
>
> Again, he sent forth other servants, saying, Tell them which are bidden, Behold, I have prepared my dinner: my oxen and my fatlings are killed, and all things are ready: come unto the marriage.
>
> But they made light of it, and went their ways, one to his farm, another to his merchandise: and the remnant took his servants, and entreated them spitefully, and slew them.
>
> But when the king heard thereof, he was wroth: and he sent forth his armies, and destroyed those murderers, and burned up their city.
>
> Then saith he to his servants, the wedding is ready, but they which were bidden were not worthy. Go ye therefore into the highways, and as many as ye find, bid to the marriage.
>
> So those servants went out into the highways, and gathered together all as many as they found both bad and good: and the wedding was furnished with guests.
>
> And when the king came in to see the guests, he saw there a man which had not on a wedding garment (who had not fabricated the Egyptian Sahu, the Solar Bodies): and he saith unto him, Friend, how camest thou in hither not having a wedding garment? And he was speechless.
>
> Then said the king to the servants, Bind him hand and foot, and take him away, and cast him into outer darkness; there shall be weeping and gnashing of teeth. For many are called, but few are chosen. - Matthew 22:1-14

The Egyptian *Book of the Occult Abode* states:

> *Go across to the farthest limits of Heaven!*
>
> *Then, just as becoming Horus, thou hast obtained a glorious body - the Sahu - (the Wedding Garment of the Soul) in like manner thou hast obtained the Crown of Nemmes.*
>
> *Indeed, thy Word of Power overtakes until the farthest limits of heaven.*
>
> *Therefore, she took possession of the divine attributes of Horus (the Being) which are those of Osiris (the Inner Logos of each one) in the region of the dead (in the region where live those who have dissolved the "I").*
>
> *Lo and behold that Horus (the Being) repeats for me the consecrated words pronounced by his Father (the Being of the Being) in the day of the funerals (of the "I"): Make the Double Lion Head God who guards the crown of Nemmes (the crown of sanctity) grant it unto thee, so that thou canst soar throughout the routes of heaven and see what exists until the furthest limits of the horizon.*
>
> *God grant me that I might be admitted into the occult secret and that the contemplation of the mystery of the birth of divinity be granted unto me. Lo and behold that Horus dresses my members with his glorious body.*

It is written in the mysterious pages of the great book of life that it is necessary to be born again in order to enter into the Kingdom of Heaven.

This is the Second Birth of which the great Kabir Jesus spoke to the Rabbi Nicodemus.

> *Except a man be born of water (semen) and of the Spirit (fire) he cannot enter into the kingdom of God.*

The Book of the Occult Abode states:

> *Lo and behold that I am born and I come into the world in the universe of Re-stau...(the Kingdom of God).*
>
> *Thanks to my priest's (or Guru's) libations in front of Osiris (the Inner Logoi), I enjoy of the blessings among the glorious "Sahu" bodies.*

I am welcome among the spirits of Re-stau (the world of the Logos) and there I grow.

To be born in the Re-stau with the Egyptian Sahu, marvellous synthesis of the solar bodies, is the extraordinary fruit of the fig tree.

This tree has been, is and always will be the living symbol of sex. Woe unto the sterile fig tree.

The Christian gospel states the following:

Now in the morning as he (the great Kabir Jesus) returned into the city, he hungered. And when he saw a fig tree in the way, he came to it, and found nothing thereon, but leaves only, and said unto it, Let no fruit grow on thee henceforward for ever. And presently the fig tree withered away.

Chapter 28

The Unconscious Itself

In accordance with Hegel, the "unconscious itself" would never have undertaken the vast and laborious task of developing the Universe, except with the hope of reaching a clear consciousness of itself.

The term "unconscious" is in its depth very ambiguous, doubtful, confusing, and discussible. However, we may use this term in a conventional way in order to indicate or point to a creative mystery, something that is much beyond the consciousness.

It is unquestionable that Parabrahman, the Universal Spirit of Life, transcends all of that which is called consciousness. Therefore, it is obvious that we may call it "Unconsciousness."

Within this strictly human theme, we can and must even emphasise the idea that before transcending the "consciousness," we first need to awaken it.

Certainly, the idea about the "absolute consciousness behind any phenomena" is extremely vague, incoherent, and imprecise.

It is absurd to confuse the consciousness with the Absolute Being. Unfortunately, many philosophers fall in those aberrations of the mind.

Sat, the Unmanifested Absolute, has nothing to do with the consciousness, because the latter, as brilliant as it might be, is like a miserable wax candle before the Uncreated Light of "That" which has no name.

Unquestionably, the Schelling and Fichte schools have become greatly severed from the archaic and primeval concept of an Absolute Principle. They have only reflected upon an aspect of the fundamental idea of the Vedanta.

The "Absoluter Geist," vaguely suggested by von Hartmann in his pessimistic philosophy about the "unconscious itself," is perhaps, in the least, the major equivalent to the European speculation in regards to the Hindu Advaitin Doctrines.

EGYPTIAN TRINITY: OSIRIS, ISIS, AND HORUS

Osiris is the Father who is in secret, the
particular Monad of every one. Isis is the
Duad, the feminine aspect of the Father,
the Divine Mother Kundalini. Horus is the
Innermost, our Divine Spirit, the Triad.

Nonetheless, it is also very distant from reality when the error is committed of identifying the Absolute Being with that which is called consciousness.

The human biped, or better if we say that homunculi who is mistakenly called human, is incapable of elaborating a single concept, unless that concept is related with completely empirical phenomena. Therefore, due to his strictly intellectual and animal constitution, he is unable to lift even the tip of the veil that covers the majesty of the Abstract Absolute Space.

The Cosmic Consciousness, the great Alaya of the Universe, must awaken within each human being. Nevertheless, we make emphasis of the necessity of not confusing the consciousness with the Absolute.

The finite cannot conceive the infinite, neither can its own type of mental experiences be applied to itself. How can it be stated that the "unconscious itself" and the Absolute itself cannot even have one instinctive impulse or hope in order to attain clear consciousness of itself?

The necessity of attaining the awakening of the consciousness is indisputable, if what we sincerely want is illumination.

Such a superlative awakening, without previously having passed through the terrible Buddhist annihilation, would be impossible. I want to emphatically refer to the destruction of the "I," to the death of the **myself**.

Two types of illumination exist.

The first one is called "Death Water" because it has bonds.

The second one is praised as "the Great Life" because it has no bonds. It is direct experience of the illuminating Void.

In order to experience in a complete way the illuminating aspect of the consciousness, we must first of all and by all means become conscious of our own selves.

It would not be possible to submerge ourselves within the current of sound, within the illuminating Void, without previously turning asunder the bonds that in one way or another bind us to the consciousness.

We transform the subconsciousness into consciousness with the annihilation of the ego. However, afterwards, we must destroy the shackles which connect us to the consciousness.

The illuminating Void is the "unconsciousness itself" (here we are utilizing the term unconsciousness in the sense of something that is far beyond the consciousness).

Have you ever heard about Anupadaka? The strict and rigorous sense of this word signifies: "without parents, without progenitors."

Osiris is the Father who is in secret, the particular Monad of every one. Isis is the Duad, the feminine aspect of the Father, the Divine Mother Kundalini. Horus is the Innermost, our Divine Spirit, the Triad.

It is easy to understand that when Horus becomes victorious in the battles against the red demons (devil "I's"), then he gives to himself the luxury of swallowing his own soul.

The best comes after this banquet. Father, Mother, and Son, in other words, Osiris, Isis, Horus, these three Divine Fires with a Diamond Soul, are mixed, fused, and integrated amongst themselves in order to form one single flame, an Anupadaka.

Therefore, the Occult Lord, the One who is immersed within the Absolute, within the inexhaustible and inconceivable Bliss, the Anupadaka, cannot have a Father, since by Himself he is Self-existent and One with the Universal Spirit of Life.

The mystery of the hierarchy of the Anupadakas within the Abstract Absolute Space is far beyond all possible comprehension for us.

Chapter 29
Green Fireballs

In these moments of worldly crisis, the modern scientists are confronting an enigma from space. I want to emphatically refer to the mystery of the green fireballs.

The green fireballs shine, sparkle, flare, then afterwards, as if they were turned off by a remote control switch, they vanish without leaving a single trace.

It has been stated to us that the residents of Albuquerque, NM are accustomed to these types of mysteries for the obvious reason of living next to the Los Alamos plant of atomic secrets.

Travellers know very well that the military forces from Sandia Base are at the edge of the city. This is the place where, for the disgrace of this afflicted world, the terrible Atomic Bomb is armed. It is evident that the famous White Sands Laboratory, specialized manufacturer of controlled remote projectiles, is located in the same state.

Nevertheless, in spite of all this secrecy, the inhabitants from that place felt bewildered; they became astonished and overwhelmed when they saw a brilliant ball of green fire silently passing through the infinite space.

"Many years ago, on a Sunday night of the past month of November, in some place of the desert which crosses through New Mexico, a mysterious event took place.

"On a clear night the stars were shining in the sky. Along the road, a Jeep was running at 25 miles per hour. This Jeep was occupied by three students from the University of New Mexico: Ted Chamberlain, student of geology, his friends Gus Armstrong, who was the owner of the jeep, and Tom Bebooy.

"It was close to nine o'clock at night. These young men were coming back from a hunting trip in San Agustin, close to Magdalena. They were carrying their hunted carcass on the back of the Jeep.

"Suddenly, the three of them became dazzled for a second. There, far away in the north-east of the sky, a gigantic ball of fire was burning while swiftly crossing the firmament.

"Its tail was off-white, yet the ball was of a radiant green color as if it was a light of a neon tube, or as Chamberlain stated, 'It was like copper when burning inside the furnace of a laboratory.'

"'Look!' Armstrong shouted at the same time that he was losing control of his jeep, which he deviated from its route. As a result, his Jeep tumbled and hurled all the occupants onto the sands of the desert.

"The ball of fire silently vanished over their heads. Minutes later, the three confused young men returned into the Jeep and went towards Albuquerque.

"Something similar happened two nights before. Lertes Miller and his wife from Palo Alto, California, were driving on road 60, close to Glove, Arizona. Then, a little before nightfall, they saw a bluish green ball which was burning up above their heads.

"Mr. Miller stated: 'It was so intense that I almost veered from the road, because I became dazzled for a few seconds.'"

A wise author stated, "This was not a common and current meteor. Observers have seen this green fire ball in the sky for many miles, from Santa Fe, New Mexico to Vista, California."

It is unquestionable and by all means it stands out that the green fire balls are absolutely different from common and current meteors.

It is evident, and observers know very well, that these balls are bigger and more luminous than the beautiful Selene (the Moon). It is obvious that not a single meteor is like that.

Their frightful and delicate silence overwhelms. It is obvious that any meteor of that size will fall with a great noise.

All of the witnesses agree that such balls move themselves in a straight line when inside of our atmosphere.

It is clear that any big or small meteor falls in a concave curve when entering into our environment.

Now, infinite conjectures exist about the mystery of these green fireballs.

"Some inhabitants from the west blame the ball for collapsing the water tower from Tucumari, New Mexico, that killed four people. This is because the investigations revealed that the fire ball passed through in the precise moments when the collapse was occurring, due to a short circuit in the lines."

Therefore, we are before a tremendous enigma and frankly we have no other choice but to return again to the Panspermia of Arrhenius (Read chapter thirteen).

"This great green fireball spectacle, which crosses the sky as lightning, is an unforgettable experience. The witnesses, as well as all of those thousands of Americans who have seen these balls in the south-east, question themselves, 'What is this?'"

The International Gnostic Movement answers this formidable question, when stating:

Electric whirlwinds, vortexes of force, escape from all planets, carrying germs of life within their bosom.

Electric whirlwinds arrive to planets carrying germs of life within their bosom.

It is obvious that now, our solar system, including our afflicted world, has arrived to a certain corner of the cosmos where these electric vortexes, carriers of vital germs, have made themselves visible.

Thus, our solar system, in its eternal journey throughout the unalterable infinite, has arrived to a corner of the universe where never expected cosmic events may occur.

THE EGYPTIAN GODDESS MAAT, WHOSE NAME MEANS "THAT
WHICH IS STRAIGHT" OR IN OTHER WORDS: "RIGHT, TRUE, TRUTH,
REAL" A MEANING IDENTICAL WITH THE SANSKRIT DHARMA.

Chapter 30
Truth-justice

During the night of mystery and within my gloomy abode, the terrible obscurity was growing from moment to moment.

My lamp was sparkling palely; it was very slowly being agonized, while its livid reflections flowed with sinister clarity.

From outside, in the street, the roughness of the inclement wind was making my windows rattle.

The rain, falling with much clattering, was lashing the glass, and when the chaos, the tempest, scratched with its lightning's sword, I then thought of the valley of darkness and the mansion of the perverse ones.

> Let my soul not to be subjugated nor dragged in captivity by the demons! Allow me to turn my face in front of the scaffold of Sepdu! (the scaffold of Karma).

> Praised be ye, oh ye planetary spirits from the constellation of the hips (Libra)!

The sacred *Book of the Occult Abode*, crying out from the profound depth of the centuries, states:

> This is in regards to you, oh divine knives of mysteries.

> "Ye, the two divine arms of the cosmic scale, which illuminate and rejoice the universe and which lead young and old men in accordance with the rhythms of the epochs, behold...!

> Behold, here is Thoth (the inner Buddha of each human being), Lord of mysteries! He precedes the libations in front of the Lord of millions of years (the Universal Logos of Life) and opens for him the way through the firmament.

> Thoth is the one who immobilizes the hurricanes and who fastens them within their forts." (He is certainly the interior Buddha of each living one, the Lord of Powers).

> Oh ye, divine Spirits of Karma, remove misery and sufferings from me! Let my soul be pleasing to Ra (God).

Hear me, humans and Gods! This firmament of steel that I had protected from the world of Amente (the region of the dead), the demon Apopi (the body of desires of every living one) has filled it with holes, since it is obvious that even the most perverse ones are accustomed to entering into that abode.

Ah, when will the people stop confusing the authentic Astral Body with the demon Apopi?

When will the pseudo-occultists comprehend that the body of desires cited by Theosophy is the frightful demon Apopi?

Common and current people do not have an Astral Body: they only have a lunar vehicle of desires, the frightful demon Apopi.

Let the humans and the dwellers of limbo hear me! Listen then! You need to build the Astral Body in the forge of the Cyclops.

Ra abhors the demon Apopi. Therefore, it is natural that every authentic Self-realized defunct one, after having dressed himself with the Egyptian Sahu, must eliminate the demon Apopi.

The Book of the Dead states the following:

> Lo and behold that I come in among the Heavenly Hierarchies, and I deliver forever Ra from the dragon Apopi."
>
> I shall watch! I shall watch! Indeed, the dragon shall not ever come nigh unto him. I shall have power over the magical signs which are placed in front of me by the demon!"
>
> I shall constantly receive sepulchral meals and the God Thoth shall provide me with the magical power which should be the outcome of my deeds (of my karma), of life bygone.
>
> I shall make Justice and Truth to go around about the bows in the heavenly boat (of my life) and I shall triumph among these Divine Hierarchies, and shall establish them (within my heart) for millions of years.
>
> The Goddess Maat (Justice) comes unto her Lord and God.

You must remember that the functions of Karma reside in the brilliant constellation of the hips (Libra)."

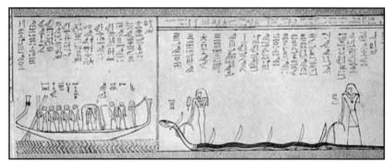

FROM THE EGYPTIAN BOOK OF THE DEAD

You must tremble in front of the divine Knives of the Law. Know that Karma is paid not only for the evil that is done, but also for the good that could be done, yet is left undone.

Remember the cycle of metamorphosis in the Boat of Khepera: the ship of our own life.

It is unquestionable that at any time it is necessary for you to descend into the Infernal Worlds, you must transform yourselves time and time again into crocodiles. It is obvious that any mystic exaltation is preceded by its correspondent humiliation. Whosoever wants to ascend must first of all descend. This is the Law.

It is indubitable that when the consciousness awakens, you transform yourselves into sparrow hawks with a human head. Thus, you can freely fly throughout starry space.

Indeed, it is evident that you must transform yourselves into Nagas, serpents. The day in which you shall be like the lotus will arrive.

> *May the Gods furnish me with thy throne, Oh Ra! furnishing me likewise with thy glorious body. I traveleth over the paths of Ra at daybreak to drive back the demon Nebt (the demon of evil will) he cometh in disguise behind a column of flames, thus on a narrow and long corridor he unexpectedly attacks me...*
>
> *Verily, relevant to the dangers expected unto me I have been warned in advance.*
>
> *I attaineth unto thy boat, Oh Ra, and behold I sitteth therein; thus, I receive the rightly deserved offerings.*

The total addition of all of those heavenly beings, namely: Elohim, Gods, Dhyan Chohans, Dhyani-Buddhas, Angels, Devas, Archangels, etc., constitute that which is commonly named God.

Chapter 31
The Homogeneous Basis

Revolutionary Gnosticism would never accept an anthropomorphic God in the style of the Biblical Jehovah, seated up above on a throne of tyranny and hurling lightning and thunderbolts against this anthill-like human swarm. Nevertheless, it is well-known that the International Gnostic Movement has never been atheistic.

Sincerely, we confess that force and forces are something very united in creation. "Gods, God exists!" exclaimed Victor Hugo...

It is obvious that variety is unity. Polytheism synthesizes itself in the unity. The total addition of all of those heavenly beings, namely: Elohim, Gods, Dhyan Chohans, Dhyani-Buddhas, Angels, Devas, Archangels, etc., constitute that which is commonly named God.

We have always believed that mortality and immortality are something extremely relative, and even when this seems to be incredible, the fact is that even God dies at the end of the Mahamanvantara.

This does not signify annihilation of that which is Divine. It is unquestionable that when the Great Cosmic Day finalizes, then the Army of the Voice, the Word, that which is called God, ceases to exist within the cosmos and goes inside the Absolute in order to be.

To be is better than to exist, and the reason for the Being to be, is to be the Being itself. Our legitimate existence is within the Absolute. This is a *not-being*, a "non-existence" to the human reasoning.

The Absolute is neither a God, nor a divine or human individual. It would be an absurdity to give form to that which has no form. It would be nonsense to try to anthropomorphize space.

Indeed, the Absolute is the unconditioned and eternal Abstract Space, very far beyond Gods and humans.

The heterogeneity unfolds itself from within the homogeneity when the dawn of the Mahamanvantara is dawning. Then, the Army of the Voice (God) is reborn again in order to create anew.

Biologists are presently searching for their homogeneous protoplasm, and chemists for their protyle, while the science of physics is laboriously searching to verify that this "force," "magnetism," "heat," etc. are all correlations of electricity.

When reaching this part of the present chapter, it is necessary that we speak a little bit more clearly. Therefore, allow me to state what I in a direct way have experienced for myself.

It is unquestionable that I have passed through the mystical experience of many previous Pralayas, because I am an Archangel of former Mahamanvantaras.

The word to better define "That" where all things originate and dissolve is without a doubt the Sanskrit word Prabhavapyaya. So, let this word be understood as a place or plane where all things originate and dissolve.

Nevertheless, it is necessary to emphasize the transcendental idea that Prabhavapyaya is neither the "Mother of the World," nor the womb of the Cosmos, nor the material cause of our planet Earth.

We, the Gnostics, found the root of the cosmos exclusively in Parabrahman and Mulaprakriti, the eternal Father-Mother, the divine Androgyne.

I cannot ever forget those moments of pleroma, those blessed moments in which the Father-Mothers taught unto their children the laws of Nature. I remember that they were instructing them with delectable songs in the language of the Light.

Therefore, it is unquestionable that the existing malleable essence in itself, the homogeneous basis of the universe, must be searched for within Parabrahman and Mulaprakriti, the One, That which is under two aspects...

While delving in this abstract subject matter that is very difficult for many to comprehend, I remember that during the profound night of Pralaya, the Father-Mothers or divine Androgynes did not easily forget the universe that existed. Therefore, when this remembrance is projected in the Abstract Absolute Space, within that which has no name, this forms paradises of inconceivable bliss.

It is indubitable that if we would pick a marvellous flower from any of those Edens of the Absolute and if afterwards we would bring it to the cosmos, it would instantaneously cease having any type of existence.

BUDDHA SHAKYAMUNI AND HIS SEVEN SERPENTS

The mutant is the outcome of a revolution
of the consciousness. It is the living product
of a psychological rebellion.

Chapter 32
Mutants

Ever since Louis Pauwels and Jacques Bergier didactically and scientifically spoke of the mutants, it is obvious to comprehend that a true ideological thoughtfulness was produced in the intellectual world.

It is unquestionable that this theme about mutants is something unusual, unexpected. Therefore, it is urgent to elucidate, to clarify, to illuminate in a meticulous way this intriguing subject matter.

Hence, delving within this vitally important subject matter, we can clearly discover two types of mutations.

We will give the classification of "favorable mutations" to the first type.

We will give the classification of "unfavorable mutations" to the second type.

Mutation is removal, change, alteration, variation. The foundation, base, support, and groundwork of the mutant is sex.

Louis Pauwels and Jacques Bergier believe that cases of authentic mutants are shown in prodigious children.

Dr. J. Ford Thomson, after having examined five thousand children in England, found among them "a bursting fury of intelligence."

Among the last ninety children of seven and nine years of age who were examined by this psychiatrist, twenty-six had an intellectual quotient of one hundred and forty, which is equivalent or close to genius.

Dr. Thomson stated that strontium ninety, a radioactive product which penetrates into the body, may be the cause of it. This product did not exist before the first atomic explosion.

The two North American sages C. Brooke and Robert K. Enrdes wrote in their distinguished book entitled *The Nature of Living Things* that they believe they can demonstrate the following: "Presently, the assemblage of genes is suffering a perturbation. As a result of this and also because of the effect of still mysterious influences, a new race of human beings endowed with superior intellectual powers is arising." This is a very daring thesis that must be accepted with a certain prudence.

It is clear by all means that the inheritance atom has been localized within the chromosomes.

It is entirely evident that the biological inheritance can be radically transformed in order to originate the mutant.

It is unquestionable that in the will for sexual transmutation and the Sahaja Maithuna, such as we taught in chapter 26 of this 1969-1970 Christmas Message, a frightful sacrifice and an authentic psychological rebellion, or better if we say, a declared insurrection against our biological inheritance exists.

The mutant is the obvious and manifested outcome of this very special type of psycho-sexual rebellion. We, the Gnostics, need to profoundly study the cardinal and definitive laws for the scientific mutation.

Any legitimate mutant of a favorable type is the specific outcome of distinct crystallizations of the Sexual Hydrogen SI-12.

It is unquestionable that the cited hydrogen represents the final outcome from the transformation of the food within the marvellous laboratory of our human organism. It is obvious that this is the primordial matter with which sex works. This is the prime substance of the Great Work, a substance which the sexual center fabricates very wisely.

It is certain that the Ens Seminis and its peculiar Hydrogen SI-12 is seed and fruit at the same time.

To transmute this portentous hydrogen, in order to give to it an intelligent crystallization on a second superior octave, actually signifies to create a new life within the existing organism, to give an evident form to the "Astral Body or Sidereal Body of the alchemists and kabbalists."

The Master "G." stated:

ENGRAVING BY MICHAEL MAIER, ATALANTA FUGIENS, 1618

"You must understand that the Astral Body is born from the same material, from the same substance, from the same matter, where the physical body is born. The only thing which is different is the procedure."

"The whole physical body, all of its cells, as a way of saying, remain impregnated by the emanations of the matter, which is SI-12. Therefore, when these have been saturated enough, then the matter SI-12 starts to crystallize."

Then the cited Master added:

"The crystallization of this matter constitutes the formation of the Astral Body."

"The transition of the matter SI-12 into a condition of emanations and into the gradual saturation of the whole organism with these emanations is what in Alchemy is called 'transmutation' or 'transformation.'"

The Master "G." continues, stating:

> "Precisely, this transformation of the physical body into the Astral Body is what in Alchemy is called the transformation of the 'gross' metals into 'fine' metals, in other words, the acquisition of gold from ordinary metals."

The scientific clue for sexual transmutation is in the Sahaja Maithuna taught in chapter 26 of this book.

The homunculi mistakenly called human being is not born with an Astral Body. It is obvious that this precious vehicle is not an indispensable implement for existing in this physical world, since the human organism possesses a vital base which allows it to live.

The Astral Body is a luxury that very few people give to themselves. An intellectual animal without such a sidereal vehicle can produce the impression of being very intelligent and even spiritual. Therefore, it is easy that in this way he can cheat himself and cheat others.

Nevertheless, there is something that the Master "G." forgot. I am emphatically referring to the demon Apopi from the Egyptian mysteries. This demon in itself is the body of desires.

It is obvious that the pseudo-esoterist and pseudo-occultist clairvoyants confuse such a demon with the precious Astral Body.

The horrible demon Apopi, base of all passional bestiality, is found in intimate relation with the Grand Sympathetic Nervous System.

Let us delve a little more within this very important theme. Let us delve into profundity, into the mind.

Allow me the freedom to disagree with the famous Dr. J. Ford Thomson. Frankly, I do not believe that those famous prodigious children, discovered by the cited psychiatrist, could be mutants.

Let us remember that the ego is memory and that it returns into new human wombs. It is unquestionable that after each death, the ego reincorporates again.

There is a vulgar statement that says: "It is not because the Devil is a devil that the Devil knows too much, but because he is very old."

In this day and age, in life, the egos are very old; they have returned into this world too many times. They have abundantly repeated what they know, what they learned. Therefore, the outcome of this repetition is the so-called "prodigious children" who are people who know their job marvellously. That is all.

The miserable homunculi falsely called human being still does not possess the authentic Solar Mind. He only has an intellectual, bestial understanding. The rational animal, even when he might be a "prodigious child," is not a mutant.

To conceive that a mutant can exist with a lunar, animal, bestial type of mind is the breaking point of absurdity. This is only possible in the mutants who are qualified as unfavorable.

Unfortunately, the great clairvoyants from the reactionary pseudo-esoterism and pseudo-occultism are also mistaken. Lamentably, they confuse the demon Hai, horror of Osiris, with the legitimate Mental Solar Vehicle.

It is unquestionable that the cited intellectual demon is the lunar, animal Mental Body which presently is occupying the human organism, the place which the authentic Christ-Mind from the favorable mutation should occupy.

The Intellectual Animal is not born with the solar type of Mental Body; he must build it if what he wants is to convert himself into a favorable mutant.

It is obvious that the Alchemist, by means of the Sahaja Maithuna, can and must transmute the Sexual Hydrogen SI-12 by passing it into a third musical octave. The outcome of such a procedure is the crystallization of that cited element into the splendid and amazing form of a supra-sensible Mental Solar Vehicle.

This is the Christ-Mind of the Gnostic Arhat, an extraordinary outcome of sexual mutation.

This specific type of mind differs very much from the animal intellect, as water differs from oil.

Another very discussible theme, which is in no way irrelevant in this chapter, is the Causal Body or Body of Conscious Will.

It is clear, obvious, and manifested that the clairvoyants from some pseudo-esoteric and pseudo-occultist systems also become lamentably mistaken about this body. This is due to the fact that they confuse the Essence with the Causal Body.

The Essence in itself is just a fraction of the Human Soul that is incarnated within ourselves. This Essence is bottled up within the ego; it is engulfed within the Lunar Bodies.

It is unquestionable that the homunculi mistakenly called human being is submitted to the Law of Recurrence. He is not capable of originating anything new; he is a victim of circumstances.

Each time that the ego returns into this valley of Samsara it repeats exactly all of the acts of its previous lives, sometimes in elevated spirals, sometimes in lower spirals.

In this day and age, within the cheap pseudo-occultism, much is spoken about the law of Epigenesis, the capacity for originating new circumstances. It is obvious that only the authentic human beings with conscious will can modify their destiny and originate a new order of things.

The Intellectual Animal has not built the Body of Conscious Will, the Causal Vehicle. The wretched, rational homunculi is always a victim of the eternal laws of Return and Recurrence.

The place within ourselves that should be occupied by the Causal Body is unfortunately occupied by the demon Nebt of the Egyptian mysteries. It is obvious that such a demon is the living personification of evil will.

We need to create the Causal Body if what we sincerely want is to incarnate the Being.

Only the Being is capable of doing. Only He can modify the circumstances and exercise with mastery the Law of Epigenesis.

Whosoever truly wants to build the Causal Body must transmute the Sexual Hydrogen SI-12 and pass it, by means of the Sahaja Maithuna, into a fourth musical octave in order to crystallize it in the excellent form of the vehicle of the Conscious Will.

The authentic mutant possesses as a fact and by his own right the four bodies: Physical, Astral, Mental, and Causal.

The vital condition for the Second Birth is to possess the four bodies of Alchemy.

Whosoever incarnates his Being reaches the Second Birth and becomes a Twice Born; he becomes a legitimate mutant.

Therefore, it is unquestionable that the type of favorable mutant is the outcome of the positive crystallizations of the Sexual Hydrogen SI-12.

Nevertheless, we must not forget that unfavorable mutants also exist. They are negative crystallizations of the Sexual Hydrogen SI-12.

I want to emphatically refer to the practitioners of Black Tantra, to those Alchemists who spill the cup of Hermes, to those who ejaculate the Ens Seminis during the Maithuna.

Those Alchemists develop the abominable Kundabuffer Organ and fortify the three traitors of Hiram Abiff and the demons of Seth within themselves.

These three traitors, Judas, Pilate, and Caiaphas, are the same three demons of the Egyptian mysteries cited in this chapter: the Demon of Desire, the Demon of the Mind, and the Demon of Evil Will.

The unfavorable mutant is found between the dilemma of disintegrating his false crystallization or entering within the submerged devolution, within the circle of the terrible necessity.

The unfavorable mutant cannot incarnate his Being within himself. He is, as a fact, a cosmic failure.

Indeed, the unfavorable mutant is a perverse homunculi, but never a true human being.

It is obvious that in order to become an authentic human being one is required to have previously built the Solar Bodies and to have incarnated the Being.

Therefore, a human being, the legitimate mutant, the true adept, is as different from the intellectual animal as the day is to night.

Radioactivity can originate the modification of the genes of certain individuals but can never create a favorable or unfavorable mutant.

The protein of the gene, slightly affected, will stop producing, as Louis Pauwels states, certain acids which are the cause of anguish. Then, we would see the appearance of cynical and perverse people who are not afraid of anything, who enjoy killing. However, these are not mutants, as some authors suppose.

The supposition of Pauwels seems ludicrous to me, that the effects of radioactivity respond to a will directed towards the heights.

It does not appear correct to me the concept that the genetic mutation produced by the atomic radioactivity of this day and age signifies a spiritual elevation for humanity.

It is obvious that the intensive radioactivity can alter the order of the genes and originate defective embryology. However, such monstrous specimens are not mutants.

We do not deny that mutation, change, and variation in a monstrous embryology exists. Nevertheless, the authentic mutant we are studying in this chapter is radically different.

The idea that a mutant is born only because of the fact of the fundamental alteration of the gene's protein seems absurd to me.

This idea of the mutant is fascinating, astonishing, and formidable. On the side of the Luciferians comes Hitler, shouting, "I am going to reveal the secret to you: The mutation of the human race has already begun. Super human beings exist."

On the side of renovated Hinduism, Pauwels stated, "The master of the Ashram from Pondichery, one of the greatest thinkers of New India, Sir Aurobindo Ghose, founded his philosophy and his sacred texts' commentaries upon the certainty of an ascending evolution of humanity performed by mutations."

We, the Gnostics, emphasise the idea that the birth of the mutant by means of atomic explosions and radioactivity cannot be possible. We do not take this Holy Communion's Parchment-Host. No one can cheat us. We can never accept the dogma of evolution.

The mutant is the outcome of a revolution of the consciousness. It is the living product of a psychological rebellion.

It seems utopian to me, the extravagant concept from Dr. Louis Wolf, English specialist in infantile sicknesses from London, when he affirms that in such a country thirty thousand phenyl-ketonic mutants are born every year.

Pauwels states that these mutants possess genes that 'he says' do not produce in their blood determined ferments which act in normal blood.

The cited author continues stating to us that a phenyl-ketonic mutant is incapable of disassociating the phenyl-alamine. Pauwels continues explaining that this incapacity makes the child vulnerable to epilepsy and to eczema. This provokes, accordingly to this cited author, a grey-ashy coloration of the hair and makes the adult person inclined towards mental sicknesses.

The mentioned author believes that this phenyl-ketonic race, separated from normal humanity, is the outcome of unfavorable mutations produced by radioactivity.

Pauwels does not want to comprehend that these sick human specimens are certainly the outcome of the atomic explosions.

It is lamentable that they make a mysticism from scientific madness, namely, from atomic experiments, H bombs, etc.

Pauwels believes in the possibility of favorable mutations by means of radioactivity from this fatal epoch in which we live. He supposes that this type of positive mutants could, 'he says,' have in their blood susceptible products in order to improve their physical equilibrium and to increase their quotient of intelligence very much above our own.

Pauwels thinks that mutants like this could carry in their veins natural sedatives that shelter them from the psychic shocks of life and from the complexes of anguish, etc., etc., etc.

It is pitiful that this otherwise intelligent author has made a religion from atomic explosions and their radiations.

Chapter 33
The Demon Hai

A long time ago, within an old palace, I found a dungeon. A venerable Elder was inside of it... His aureole beard had thirteen clusters of hair, his white head had thirty-one long curls of hair.

He was the Ancient of Days, Goodness of the Goodness, Concealed of the Concealed, Mercy of Mercies.

His neck was like a tower of ivory, his eyes like the fish-pools in Heshbon by the gate of Bath-rabbim, his nose was as the tower of Lebanon which looks towards Damascus...

Then, I fell on my knees biting the dust of the earth! And while holding a dagger in my hand, I shouted with anguish... I exclaimed with all the strength of my soul, "I killed him! I killed him!"

Strange vision... The years passed by; the days of my wild youth were gone. Then, finally, I understood.

It is written with fiery letters within the book of the law that the fallen Bodhisattvas enter into the cycle of the terrible necessity accused of three crimes:

First: To have assassinated their Buddha.

Second: To have dishonored the Gods.

Third: Many other different, common and current crimes.

I was a fallen Bodhisattva. Yes! Yes! Yes! It is unquestionable that if I had not repented, I would have entered into the submerged devolution of the mineral kingdom...

Have you ever heard of the Count Zanoni? Like him, I also had an immortal, physical body.

In the ancient continent Mu, after the departure from Eden, I, with my heart contrite, re-entered into the Mysteries.

I swallowed soil...! Yes! Yes! Yes! My body was entombed, the Gods know this...

The Initiatic Resurrection came after three days. I utilized the fourth dimension in order to escape from the sepulchre...

The Holy Women treated my Lemurian body with many medicines and aromatic ointments...

During the course of more than ten thousand years of incessant earthquakes and erupting volcanoes, that ancient continent Mu was submerging itself within the boisterous waters of the Pacific Ocean.

Nevertheless, I continued to exist with my immortal body on the Atlantean continent. I led many mystical peregrinations that went sometimes towards Yucatan or to Tehotihuacan.

To achieve the immortality of the human organism would seem more than impossible for the people who are not versed in revolutionary Gnosticism. Present sages particularly want to achieve this, but it is obvious that they do not know our formulae.

I confess that in that epoch, I especially liked very much to abide in a precious valley now covered by the stormy waters of the Gulf of Mexico.

The Fourth Root Race or Atlantean Race notably evolved until reaching its objective. Then subsequently, it precipitated itself through the devolving, descending path. It is obvious that a descent always occurs after every ascent; an ascension is always followed by a descent.

When the continent that was known with the name of Atlantis was submerged within the Atlantic ocean, some survivors continued to exist in present lands, as the studies of palaeontology have already started to suspect.

I want to emphatically refer to two types of people.

The first ones were the famous troglodytes, who were Atlanteans in a decisively devolving state. Obviously, they were submerged within the most frightful barbarian state, such as the occidental science has discovered when finding their unmistakable remains within the profound caverns of the earth.

The second ones were Atlanteans in an evolving state. These historic Pelasgians were very educated people who, from the first igneous manifestations of the second Transapalnian catastrophe, initiated their return towards the oriental regions that were their place of origin.

This is the origin of the universal tradition of the Exodus of IO from the Garden of Hesperides (Poseidon), throughout all meridional Europe and through Bosphorus, towards Colchis and Armenia where, in accordance with tradition, the Ark of Noah was docked or where the Holy Initiatic Cult of Ar-ar-at or Cult of the Arian mountains where the Tigris and Euphrates and other rivers are born, was established.

A wise esoterist author stated:

> "These Pelasgians or Occidental Ario-Atlanteans received a different name in each one of the regions of the world where they were spread out.
>
> "They were called Cyclops because they had the eye of intuition still opened, since they were more or less depositaries of the Initiatic Truths. The gigantic constructions that they built were labelled Cyclopean constructions.
>
> "It is clear that from the North American Pennsylvania until the Oxus and the Aral throughout Europe and Africa still such astonishing constructions in ruin are shown.
>
> "They were called Tyrians and Titans because of the God It or Ti, or Hercules who was commanding them. Regarding Hercules, there exists a more abundant amount of data than what is believed to exist.
>
> "They were called Kalcas or Chaldeans or Chalcidians because of their ante-Atlantean origin from the Kalcas country, which they used to return to, also because of knowing the Copper (Calcas) and because of developing themselves in an age of frank decadency.
>
> "They were called Akkadians because of their navigating knowledge and because of having passed through the sea with their redeemers, their leaders.

"They were called Arkkadians, which was a deviation from Akkadians, or it was a reference to the Ark or symbolic boat that recalled them.

"They were called Colchidians or Colchians as a deviation of the word calchis (knowledge of numeration, or the Hieratic-hieroglyphic and symbolic writing, Kabbalah, etc.).

"They were called Aramaeans or Arian men, Druids because of their Initiated Priests and because of their fire cult, that is to say, their cult to the Sun, to Purity, to the Truth buried in the catastrophe.

"They were called Janos because of their Inca-Conductor or King Priest (IAO, TAO, IANUS etc.). They were called Bretons or Brittanys from Brig (Bright), the Arian radical sign from that which shines, which glows, in other words, always and forever the Sun.

"They were called Menfires or Menhirs because they were occidental people, or more commonly because of their fire cult. Thus, they named themselves and even the stones of their sepulchres Men-Hirs.

"They were called Nahoas, Nahuales in Mexico and in certain parts of Arabia, Syria, etc., and Nebo, the Initiatic Wisdom.

"They were called Tuathas of Danand, for the same or similar reasons, already explained in another part.

"They were called Sumerians (from Suria the sun), in Babylon and Nineveh, and Ti Huan Ascos or Ti Huanacos in Peru.

"They were called Thessalian primitives, maybe because of the expressed retrocession of their peregrinations.

"They were called Myneans, because of their colonization in the Island of Crete, and Mycenaeans because of other islands similar in Asia minor and Greece.

"They were called Germanos because of the God Hermes, Toth or Odin, Ercinians from 'ERDA' the Mother Earth.

"They were called Sabaeans, because of their Wisdom in heavenly and terrestrial things.

"They were called Hemiarits or Homerits because of their double Aryan and Atlantean character (origin), from their epoch and country of colonisation.

"They were called Camits because of their instructor Cam, Jan or Janos, Hyperboreans because of the regions where the Greeks knew them and because of the White Island beyond the Boreas and because of their most excellent Initiatic traditions from the First Root Race.

"They were called Axinos or inaccessible ones in the Jinn concept: Phrygians from the Scandinavian Goddess Phrygia, Juno or Diana-Lunus.

"They were called Missios or 'Envoys' in order to save the Troglodyte humanity from its definitive physical and moral ruin.

"They were called Taurines because of their Mythraic cult, which gave the name unto the celebrated Armenian mountain range.

"They were called Phallegeans as eternal, peregrines or errant human comets, Curetes and Quiretes because of their quiritarian (Kyries, Lance, Sun-Beam) acts and because of their Caurias or Curias, Aenians or Aeonians because of their Aeneas, Enos, Enoch, Janos or Noah."

It was precisely in the Oriental World, during that brilliant Ario-Atlantean epoch, when I committed an error similar to that one committed by the count Zanoni.

He fell in love with a beautiful artist from Naples. Thus, the outcome was frightful because he died under the guillotine during the French Revolution.

Count Zanoni was an immortal Chaldaean. He received the Elixir of Long Life in ancient times and it is clear to comprehend that sex was forbidden to him.

My case was similar; I was an ancient Lemurian with an immortal body. I also fell in the arms of Kundry, that Eve from

Hebraic Mythology, the woman of antonomasia. Hence, the outcome was the fatal loss of my precious Lemurian vehicle.

It is written with characters of fire in the book of life that any Resurrected Master must not return to sex.

This is known by the divine and humans. The violation of this great law signifies death.

It is evident that my capital error was that I accepted the gift of Cupid at the height of my youth.

Therefore, I tell human beings and Gods that they should always avoid immortalizing a young physical body.

When the civilization of the First Aryan Subrace flourished in the central plateau of Asia, I intended to re-emerge. Then, I entered with much humbleness into the Sacred Order of Tibet. This is how I became an authentic Lama.

I had to build the Solar Bodies again by means of the Sahaja Maithuna.

It is written in the Akashic records of Nature that I then re-conquered the Second Birth.

Unfortunately, I committed certain extremely grave mistakes when I wanted to help the Queen of my country with the Sacred IT Clue.

I was expelled from this Venerated Order due to this mistake. I then continued in Samsara.

I returned into Egypt during the dynasty of the Pharaoh Kephren. I achieved a lot then, but not everything.

Presently, after having suffered a lot, I have returned onto the straight path. Now, I am standing (on my feet) anew.

I know in depth the path of the Revolution of the Consciousness. Therefore, this is why I am the Avatar of the New Aquarian Age.

All the intellectual homunculi, mistakenly called human beings, solely wish to liberate themselves from death. However, they do not know how to liberate themselves from life.

Blessed be the ones who are dignified by the glacial beauty of the blessed Goddess Mother Death.

Blessed be the ones who destroyed the illusory wall of their vain existence, those who dissolved the "I," and who were within all of the abysses.

Death! That which was our whole yesterday, today is just our nothingness...! Eternity! Sepulchral beauty..!

I wept a lot, I descended into the Forge of the Cyclops, I shouted with the whole strength of my soul: "Hear my imploring voice, oh Isis! Tear thy cowl... and thy unknowable star...! Have pity on me, make me a sign of light..."

"Eternity: return to me what thou tookest from me: my purple tunic, my wedding garments...!

"Abyss from a profound mystery: reimburse me that which thy deepness absorbed! Sphinx from the desert of Egypt: Open thine ear...! Have pity now, oh obscure night..."

What seas without shores, what an infinite night, what profound wells, what Stygian beasts I found within the interior of myself...!

Thus, I returned to the Second Birth dressed with the Wedding Garment of the soul. Thus, I learned how to die within myself.

Now, I am a defunct one who can tranquilly study *The Book of the Dead.*

I am alive, nonetheless, I am dead...

Ah...! If people could understand all of this...

Hence, that night on which I returned into the Sacred Order of Tibet, I was happy. I left the cadaver of the terrible demon Apopi within the deepest abysses.

Lord! Lord! How much I suffer when I see these mistaken, wretched people! They think that they already possess the Astral Body. However, they truly only possess the body of desires, the abominable demon Apopi...

Beautiful work from my Mother Kundalini...! She reduced the frightful Demon of Desire into dust...

But what about the mind...? Woe! Woe! Woe!... Alas! How terribly proud I was with my mental demon, with the frightful devil Hai... I also believed that this was the authentic intellectual vehicle...

Oh, God of mine! The *causa causarum* of my lunar mental vehicle was lust... This is how I comprehended it...

If I would have known it before... Yes! Yes! Yes! I knew it, but I forgot.

I open the Egyptian *Book of the Occult Abode* and I study chapter XL, which literally states:

> Get thee hence oh Demon Hai! (Demon of the Mind) horror of Osiris. Thine head (the mental lunar vehicle) has been cut by Thoth (Buddha, the Innermost). The cruelties (the work on mental disintegration) that I have exercised on thyself, has been commanded unto me by the Hierarchies of heaven.
>
> Get thee hence, then, oh demon Hai, thou unto whom Osiris feels horror! Get away from my boat (my life's own ship) blown by propitious winds.
>
> Gods from heaven who have demolished the enemies of Osiris (those entities or devil "I"s that constitute the ego), watch!
>
> The Gods from the vast land are subjugated. Away from me demon AM-AAU, (Hai), the God, Lord of the region of the Dead (Initiates) detest thee!
>
> I know thee! I know thee! I know thee! Away from me, demon (of the animal mind), do not attack me, since I am pure and I accommodate myself unto the cosmic rhythms.
>
> Do not approach me (do not tempt me), thou who comest without being invited! Thou dost not know me, demon (who thinks that he knows everything) who ignores that I conserve the dominion over the enchantments of thy mouth (which speaks grandeur, but does not know anything)!
>
> Therefore, know this! Although, it seems that I am at the shelter of thy claws. In regards to thee, oh demon HAS-AS! (the same demon of the mind), behold Horus (the divine Spirit of each person) who cuts thy claw (the time).
>
> Verily he has been destroyed in Pe and in Dep (the worlds of desire and of the mind) with his legions of demons (devil-"I"s) in the battlefield array.

*It has been the eye of Horus (clairvoyance) who by studying
thee and seeing thee has defeated thee, (but with the help of Isis).*

*I reject thee demon, in accordance with thy advances! I have
defeated thee by means of the breath of my mouth (the Word),
I have defeated thee who tortures the sinners and who devours
them (perverse mind).*

*Therefore, give back unto me my writing tablet with all of
the accusations which it contains (blasphemous and accusing
mind). I have not committed sins against the Gods, therefore do
not attack me.*

*Take just what I, myself grant thee (the death which thou
deserves: the abyss).*

*Do not take me with thee. Do not devour me! Since I am the
Lord of Life, Sovereign of the Horizon (an already Christified
Being).*

So, this is how, by intensely working and by supplicating
Isis, my Divine Mother Kundalini, I finally achieved the
disintegration, the reduction of the terrible demon Hai of the
Egyptian Mysteries into cosmic dust.

Such a perverse demon is the very same mental body that
many authors wrote about, namely: Leadbeater, Annie Besant,
Max Heindel, Arthur Power, etc. Frankly, I do not blame those
authors, since they did what they could. Wretched ones... They
suffered a lot... ... ...

Nevertheless, we, the brethren of the Gnostic Movement,
have to delve into the root of all these things, and this is not a
crime.

Jesus the great Kabir stated:

*Suffer little children and forbid them not, to come unto me; for
of such is the kingdom of heaven.* - Matthew 19:14

It is urgent to re-conquer the infancy in the mind, in the
heart, and in the sex. To intend such a re-conquest without
previously eliminating the lunar mental body (demon Hai)
would be an absurdity.

Such an intellectual, animal vehicle is a granulated Luciferian
fire. It is obvious that the origin of the animal mind was lust.

The most tremendous ordeal was also the decisive one. One given night, my own Innermost God, by placing a crucible filled with Liquid Mercury on the floor, intended to verify an alchemical transmutation, but because there was no fire under the crucible, it is obvious that he failed in his intent.

Then, he made me to understand that he needed to perform such an alchemical operation with the purpose of crystallizing a new, extremely subtle organism. I believed that maybe it was related with the creation of the famous Sambogakaya, that in accordance with some high Initiates, it is stated that it has three more perfections than the ineffable vehicle of the Nirmanakayas.

Well... I am a Nirmanakaya, and it is clear that by having the possibility of possessing the precious vehicle of the Sambogakayas was something extremely tempting for me.

"I have failed in this operation because of the lack of fire," said my real Being unto me. Then, he added "Give me a match" (spark, ember or flame). I understood that I should perform a work of Sexual Magic.

This left me perplexed, confused, astonished... Yes...

But, is it perhaps licit for a Twice Born one to return into the flaming forge of Vulcan? What is this? What? What?

It is clear that I did not fail in this ordeal... That night other Adepts were submitted to the same ordeal. Some of them failed, others did not fail...

The fact that the very Innermost God submits oneself to ordeals is certainly rare and astonishing.

By all means it stands out that the Beloved One wants to be sure of that which he possesses. He needs a Diamond Soul (Vajrasattva).

The reception in the temple was formidable. The venerable Ancient of Days (my Monad) and I, wretched suffering soul, grasped with our right hands: He the Sceptre and I the Cross...

Both of us entered into the sanctuary revested with our sacred vestures...

I knew that I had assassinated this Elder but He had resuscitated within me: "The King is dead, long live the King..."

Nevertheless, I was not the one, wretched soul in pain, who had assassinated the Ancient of Days...

The three traitors, Judas, Pilate, and Caiaphas killed him... Yes... Yes... Yes...

However, it is obvious that Pilate always washes his hands. How horrible is Hai, the Demon of the Mind!

Thus, inside the temple and in front of the altar, the Elder of all ages and I were praying...

The Elder placed very close a Buddhic bowl filled with coins... These coins in themselves are capital of good deeds...

It is clear that my good deeds were enough in order to pay the old and to acquire forgiveness.

The final festivity was marvellous, portentous. This was performed in a splendid hall.

The host was a glorious Master of the White Brotherhood... Some trees within that precious hall were crowned with laurels... Those small bushes were looking very beautiful in their pots; they were standing out within that hall.

All the guests arrived with funeral attire and with very much respect, since they had to celebrate the defunct's festivity...

The horrible demon Hai had died. Therefore, this deserved a festivity... Soon that hall was filled with people...

I greeted many guests... The Host-Master welcomed many others...

The delightful music and the tables filled with people gave to the place a very special note of cosmic happiness.

I felt joyful when conversing with the great Hierophant...

Now, I do not have Lunar Mind. Nevertheless, I can think; I use my Solar Mind, the one that I built in the forge of the Cyclops (sex).

THE WHEEL OF SAMSARA (BHAVA CHAKRA) WHOSE OUTER RING ILLUSTRATES THE
TWELVE NIDANAS OR LINKS OF DEPENDENT ORIGINATION (PRATITYASAMUTPADA).

Chapter 34
The Causes of Existence

We can and must classify the multiple causes of existence in three orders:

1. Physical causes

2. Metaphysical causes

3. Karmic causes

The first cosmic order of causality has already been studied, even though in a superficial way, by the men of the official science.

The second causal cosmic order has been very deeply investigated by oriental sages.

The third causal cosmic order has been scrutinized with the open Eye of Dangma by the Jivanmukta or Self-realized Adepts.

All the known physical laws, like gravitation, cohesion, weight, etc., are included within the first category.

The desire of living in this physical world, the longing for sentient life, which is a manifested result of the Nidanas and Maya (illusion), are very hidden within the second causal category.

The Laws of Action and Consequence are found within the third category. There is no effect without a cause...

Before the dawn of the Mahamanvantara, the two first causal orders were destroyed.

If the third order would have been destroyed, then the Solar Universe within which we live, move, and have our Being, would never have been born in the infinite space.

It is unquestionable that any planet or solar system that comes into cosmic existence is the outcome of Karma...

Yonder, in the preterit solar system, which is now represented by all the moons of our present solar system of Ors, the Gods intensively worked and even had their mistakes...

The Gods also commit mistakes...

The worlds of the past solar system are now cadavers, moons,...

Each one of the present planets from our solar system is related with these moons...

The Earth is no exception... This is known by the divine and humans...

The Earth is a living reincarnation of the lunar soul... This is known by any Mahatma.

Unfortunately, and as a breaking point of woes, our terrestrial planetary fire is very poor and is charged with lunar karma...

This is due to the fact that the fruits of such a fire were formerly very poor in the lunar world. This is how it is written in the book of the Law.

We have this karmic outcome visible in this valley of tears. Indeed, this terrestrial humanity is a lost case... You know this...

If the Gods had not owed cosmic karma, then the Earth and the whole solar system of Ors presently would not exist.

Before the dawn of the Great Day, the invisible which is and the visible which was remained within the eternal Not-Being, the Unique-Being.

Chapter 35
Atomic Bombs in Orbit

Russia is organizing a spatial horror. The sound note of caution was given in Washington. They said that these infernal atomic loads can be detonated by remote control.

This very unpleasant Machiavellian system of horror consists of a series of atomic bombs in orbit, which are abominable, execrable, and horrifying.

Indeed, life upon the face of the earth is now becoming almost impossible. Now, the evil of the world overflows and has reached to heaven.

Indeed, this is "not a very beautiful intention" from the Kremlin, which is to place in motion their monstrous program denominated "Fractional System for Orbital Bombing."

The dreadful "SFOB" bombs indeed are neither a beautiful caress or a demonstration of love for this wretched suffering humanity.

Once in orbit, such nuclear bombs would be placed at a very low height, about 160 kilometers above the earth, and it is obvious that before they could complete their first circuit, they would be detonated by remote control against military objectives and defenseless cities.

It is indubitable that these horrendous "SFOB" bombs would fatally navigate a fraction of an orbit before its detonation.

The lower altitude would give to these devices the possibility of not being detected by the swift, watchful radar system possessed by the United States of America.

We have been notified that the Russians have carried with success at least thirteen scientific SFOB-type experiments.

It has been said to us that the initial seven orbital atomic experiments failed, but "they said" that the following six ones were a complete success.

This very unpleasant Machiavellian system of horror
consists of a series of atomic bombs in orbit, which
are abominable, execrable, and horrifying.

It is obvious that the Yankees (U.S.A.) are not meek sheep either. Thus, we can be absolutely sure that not only will they imitate Russia's example, but moreover, they probably will invent something worse.

A Soviet Minister threateningly shouted about a pacific co-existence or atomic war. Unfortunately, "Tyrians" and "Trojans" hate peace and this is already demonstrated with clear, blunt, and definitive facts.

In these instants of world crisis and demographic explosions, alarming symptoms of world war exist everywhere.

The radioactive particles from nuclear explosions will profoundly alter the superior zones of our terraqueous atmosphere.

It is obvious (this is known by any scientist) that such zones constitute something like a supreme filter for the solar rays.

When such a marvellous filter is completely altered by the filthy nuclear explosions, then unquestionably, the atmosphere will not be able to filter, analyze, and decompose the solar rays into light and heat. Therefore, the result will be that we will see the sun "black as a sackcloth of hair." [Revelation 6:12]

It is important to know that the superior layer of the planetary atmosphere is the living support of our world and that its alteration will cooperate in the intensification of earthquakes and seaquakes.

Then the cities will breakdown, turn into dust, and maritime waves (tsunamis) never seen before will lash the shores.

It is written in the Christian Gospel that a very strange sound will emerge from within the very bottom of the seas.

Unknown sicknesses, never discovered before by medical science, are already appearing as a consequence of atomic abuse.

The phosphorus of the human brains will be contaminated by the radiations and many people will lose their reasoning and will go mad around the streets. Hospitals will be loaded with sicknesses and there will be no relief.

It is evident that the waters of the earth and heaven will be also contaminated. Therefore, the harvests will be lost. These will not be utilized by the hungry multitudes due to the fact that the crops will be contaminated by atomic radiation.

Then, we will see horrifying Dantesque scenes around the streets, and amidst the smoky ruins of this perverse civilization of vipers we will only hear wailing, howling, whistling, neighs, squeaks, bellows, gaggles, meows, barking, snorts, snoring, and croaks.

Chapter 36

The Demon Nebt

The infinite and I were found face to face. The divine clouds from the west were like a horde of formless dogs chasing a cloud of Titans. Thus, within that scarlet purple deepness, ineffable things were shown...

Suddenly, the obscure frieze became illuminated by the sun, so its goldenness, internal and delicate, sidereal and pure, broke asunder into exquisite splendours, with mysterious moonlike paleness that slowly vanished within a placid opalescent and silvery vision...

Then, I abandoned my dense body, and dressed with the wedding garment of the soul, I entered into the Superior Worlds.

What subsequently happened in those regions of *One Thousand and One Nights* is well-known by the Gods...

I saw myself delectably lying down in a royal nuptial chamber. It was love's hour. Thus, all of the waves of rivers, fountains, and seas sung in an ineffable chorus, preluding a rhythm from the *Song of Songs*.

The blessed incense from the exhaled perfume of all flowers was floating as an enchantment. This was irradiated within the zephyrs, which with the humming of their wings, were assaying a concert of kisses and sighs...

It was the nuptial hour. Nature, coming out from chaos, still dazzled, inebriated with youth and beauty, virginal and sacred, veiling herself in mystery, was smiling...

"Kiss me, my love," said to me the Eve of Hebrew mythology, or Kundrigia, Herodias, the woman as a symbol...

"I will kiss thee as a sister with a sacred osculum. I abhor animal passion, thou knowest it..."

The dense forest, having the presentiment of the new day, was covering its wooded grounds with rumors. The happy and playful water was running away among canes and trembling reeds, while the Angel of the mist was shaking the miraculous drops of his wings upon the flowers...

It was the nuptial hour. The land from *One Thousand and One Nights* was sleeping as a delectable virgin under her chaste veil, and when the divine sun as a lover surprised her in order to kiss her with sanctity, he illuminated heaven...

Thus, bathed in splendor, filled with the dawning, I abandoned the royal nuptial chamber and went out with her...

We walked slowly... slowly... slowly... until the edge of an old precipice... "Be careful!" exclaimed the maiden-spouse...

I answered, "Do not be afraid...! The danger is not here, it has already passed by. The danger was really there, inside in the nuptial chamber... It is not the ending of which you have to be afraid, but the beginning, whose outcome becomes this abyss."

Hence, after uttering these words with a voice which surprised even my own self, the maiden-lover from that delectable ordeal disappeared, as a dint of magic ...

Then, the Beloved One (Atman), my real Self, the Innermost, the Secret Master, came unto me...

The Blessed One joyfully advanced towards me in the act of teaching me and greeting me at once...

The Venerable One came attired with the sacred garment of the Principalities... His steps were preceded by my Spiritual Soul (Buddhi), who was also attired with the same vesture...

I, the wretched human soul (the Causal or Superior Manas of Theosophy), joyfully embraced my twin sister (Buddhi)... The Blessed One was staring at us and smiling...

Ah...! I said unto myself... I must eliminate the frightful Demon of Evil-Will from my own interior nature. This demon is the horrifying Nebt of the Egyptian mysteries. Thus, only by doing this can I earn the right to use the sacred vesture that I see on my sister and on my Beloved One.

> May the Gods furnish me with thy throne, Oh Ra!, furnishing
> me likewise with thy glorious body. I traveleth over the paths of
> Ra at daybreak to drive back the demon Nebt (the Demon of
> Evil Will) he cometh in disguise behind a column of (passional)

flames, thus on a narrow and long corridor (of esoteric ordeals) he unexpectedly attacks me...

Verily, relevant to the dangers expected unto me, I have been warned in advance.

I attaineth unto thy boat, Oh Ra, and behold I sitteth therein; thus, I receive the rightly deserved offerings. (This is textually taken from *The Book of the Dead* of ancient Egypt.)

"...On earth, peace towards men of good will..." If people could understand what this phrase signifies... If they could learn how to perform the will of the Father...

If they could intentionally dissolve the demon Nebt, the Devil of Evil Will... Then, the earth would become an Eden... Each one would learn to respect the free will of his neighbors...

Nevertheless, woe! Woe! Woe!... Everything in this world is lost. All of the human beings want to dominate their neighbors, they want to climb, to show themselves off on the top of the ladder, to boast of themselves...

The abominable demon Nebt powerfully reigns upon the face of the earth...

Therefore, during those disquieting days of intensive esoteric work, I had to study this sinister Demon of Evil Will very deeply. I am referring to the terrible Nebt.

It is written that any intellectual animal carries inside the horrendous Caiaphas, the third traitor of Hiram Abiff.

If Judas, the dreadful Demon of Desire, the abominable Apopi, is thus so depraved, if Pilate the tenebrous one of the mind, the hideous devil Hai, causes us too much pain with his indignant justifications and washing of hands, then, what can we say about the horrendous Caiaphas?

I saw my own (Demon of Evil-Will) climbing up step after step throughout the stairs of my own abode. It is unquestionable that he possessed a Caesarean, impotent, and terrible aspect...

To reduce into cosmic dust this perverse Demon of Evil Will is only possible with the power of the Divine Mother Kundalini, the igneous serpent of our magical powers.

It was necessary for me to study in a detailed way all of these occult concomitances.

To penetrate many times into the region of natural causes (into the world of Conscious Will) with the evident purpose of investigating mysteries, was urgent for me...

Hence, I navigated within the profound chaotic waters of the infinite space and I saw and heard extraordinary things, which for the wretched, rational animals are impossible to comprehend.

It is clear that in a state of perfect lucidity (in the world of Conscious Will), I received direct information about the work...

Then, I comprehended in an integral way the displeased attitude of many people who unjustly are wrathful with me, just because I do not accept their theories. Woeful creatures...!

During a very deep Samadhi, I saw many boats with white sails which were adorned with multiple diamond signs...

Crosses, roses, diamantine stars were adorning the mystic boats of that profound ocean...

Solar boats, Mahatmas, Diamond Souls, Jivanmuktas, Mahatmas, navigate within the waters of the chaos...

"When one is very close to God, one must be very prudent." Whosoever eliminates the third traitor of Hiram Abiff is converted into a Diamond Soul...

The Egyptian *Book of the Occult Abode* states:

> I, Osiris, hold a threat over the tempest of heaven. I wrap with bandages and fortify Horus, the good God, continuously (by means of the esoteric work).

> I, whose forms are diverse and multiple, receive my offerings in the hours established by fate. The tempests are immobilised in front of my rostrum. Behold that Ra (the Logos) arrives accompanied by four superior divinities. Everybody sails in heaven on the Solar Boat. I, Osiris, I depart on my journey at the hour established by fate. Thus, mounted upon the cordage of the Solar Boat (or Diamond Boat), I begin my new existence.

Chapter 37
The Seven Cosmocreators

Christic esoterism mentions the seven creator spirits in front of the throne of the Lamb. Therefore, it is important to clarify this matter and to place at once the cards on the table.

These seven cosmocreators are the same Dhyan Chohans who clearly correspond to the Hebrew Elohim. The cosmic order is the following:

1. Moon: Regent Gabriel

2. Mercury: Regent Raphael

3. Venus: Regent Uriel

4. Sun: Regent Michael

5. Mars: Regent Samael

6. Jupiter: Regent Zachariel

7. Saturn: Regent Orifiel

It is unquestionable that the Dhyanis successively watch each one of the seven rounds and root races of our planetary chain.

It is obvious that each one of the seven emanates from himself his own human soul, that is to say, his Bodhisattva, when it is necessary.

It is indubitable that any one from the seven can send his Bodhisattva anywhere.

I, personally, am the Bodhisattva of Samael, the fifth of the seven, and any esoterist knows that I am the one who has suffered the most.

My real innermost Being is in himself an Osiris, Isis, Horus, Iod-Heve, the Heart of Heaven in accordance with the Mayan *Popol Vuh*, Adam Kadmon, Brahma-Viraj, etc., etc., etc.

Before unfolding himself into the Duad and into the Triad, my real innermost Being is the Pythagorean Monad, the Unique-One, the Buddhist Aunad-Ad, the Ain Suph, En Soph or Chaldaean Pneuma-Eikon, etc., etc., etc.

However, in regards to myself, I am the Bodhisattva of the Lord, the Innermost. I do not ever pretend to boast of being perfect.

My duty is to teach the Fifth Truth, the Fifth Gospel, the Fifth Veda. It is not necessary to wait for the coming of the Fifth Round, as many believe, in order for my doctrine to be known.

Here you have my doctrine. Therefore, whosoever hears my voice and follows it, I will liken him unto a wise man who built his house upon the living rock, and the floods and tempests came and beat upon that house; and it fell not: for it was built upon a solid foundation.

Yet, whosoever rejects my word can certainly be compared unto a foolish man who built his house upon the sand, and the rivers and anguished tempests came and beat upon that house; and it fell into the precipice with a great noise: for it had not a solid foundation.

I can never deny that I have been with this terrestrial humanity since the dawn of creation.

My Father who is in secret is perfect, but it is unquestionable that I, his Bodhisattva, cannot show off any perfections...

By no means would I commit a sin of immodesty if I emphatically affirm that I have been a witness of the nightfall and dawning of various Mahamanvantaras (Cosmic Days).

My duty is to give testimony of all that I have seen and heard. This humanity needs with urgency a legitimate orientation.

During the Mahamanvantara of Padma or Lotus of Gold, I accomplished in the Lunar World a very similar mission to the one that in these instants I am accomplishing on this planet Earth.

I taught the Selenites the Fifth Truth; yet, it is obvious that it was rejected by a unanimity of votes.

The outcome was death on the cross. It is obvious that whosoever becomes a redeemer dies crucified.

Some few Selenites accepted the Fifth Gospel. These ones, after hard work, became Self-realized in depth and converted themselves into Angels.

It is written in the great book of life that at the end of that Lunar Apocalypse, a new group accepted the doctrine. Therefore, another planetary abode was given to those repented ones, where presently they are Self-realizing themselves.

Any Mahatma can verify for himself with his open Eye of Dangma that those Selenite multitudes who formerly pronounced themselves against the Fifth Gospel, presently live in an underground world. They converted themselves into authentic Lucifers.

At the end of the seventh round of the Lunar Chain, the virginal sparks, rays, or divine lightning bolts submerged themselves within the Absolute without any Self-realization, save some few exceptions. These were the Men-Angels who indeed accepted the doctrine.

When the failed virginal sparks submerged themselves within the uncreated light of the Abstract Absolute Space, they radically abandoned their tenebrous ex-personalities who were violently precipitated through the devolving path...

It is obvious that such sinister ex-personalities or Lucifers continue devolving, going backwards, descending into the infernal worlds. They slowly descend throughout the animal, vegetal, and mineral stages. Only the Second Death can liberate these souls. Thus, they can eventually restart the ascension, from the mineral to the human being.

It is then absolutely false to asseverate that at the end of a Mahamanvantara (Cosmic Day), all of the living beings attain the state of Paranishpanna or Absolute Perfection. "Yon-grub," radical perfection, is never the outcome of the evolving mechanics.

The revolution of the consciousness is another thing. However, this is an unpleasant thing for everybody... You know this...

Jesus, the great Kabir, stated:

> If any man will come after me, let him deny himself, and take up his cross, and follow me. - Matthew 16:24

"To deny himself" signifies to dissolve the pluralized "I."

"To take up his cross," which by itself is one hundred percent phallic, factually signifies a sexual crossing, to work in the flaming forge of Vulcan with the evident purpose of achieving the Second Birth.

To follow the Intimate Christ signifies sacrifice, to be willing to give even the last drop of blood for this suffering humanity.

So, the end of a Mahamanvantara does not include the realization of the Innermost Self of all creatures.

Therefore, while holding my hand over my heart, I can tell you that it is very difficult to find Self-realized people.

We, all of the human bipeds, are more or less demons. To stop being demons, to convert ourselves into something different, distinct, is something that corresponds to the Mysteries.

Nevertheless, why would something be given to people that they do not want, if they, the multitudes are happy with the way they are, if they do not wish to be different? Therefore, neither the evolving mechanics, nor even the twilight of the Mahamanvantara could compel them to be distinct.

The radical change, the realization of the Innermost Self, is the outcome of a series of frightful super-efforts performed on and inside ourselves here and now.

Therefore, to achieve a radical change, a definitive trans-formation, is only possible based on tremendous self-efforts.

It would be an absurdity to suppose for even a moment that the in depth change, the authentic interior Self-realization, could be the outcome of an involuntary and mechanical way, as the fanatics of the dogma of evolution think.

So long as a human being does not achieve the state of Anupadaka, it is absolutely impossible for him to experience the nature of Paranirvana.

The true nature of Paranirvana was publicly taught up until the days of the Yogacharya school. However, since then, this doctrine was kept in secret, since it is obvious that the rational homunculi are not prepared in order to comprehend it.

Chapter 38
Cancer

What is cancer...? We answer this question by emphasizing the idea that it is the disorderly and anarchical development of the cells of the patient's own organism.

Is cancer contagious? The scientific experiments made in the Institute for Experimental Medicine of Argentina were conclusive. The scientists placed sick rats and healthy rats in the same cage. Unquestionably, they did not discover any type of contagion. Rats of different sexes have been placed within such properly controlled experiments and have been found without contagion. It has been stated in the scientific world that rats that were fed with cancerous tumors did not become infected. They affirm that rats that were injected with the blood of a sick animal remained immune, without contagion.

Can any type of wound cause cancer? This type of question has an extraordinary importance, from the civil point of view and from the legal point of view, because of the claims that could be made for compensation of work accidents. These claims could be attributed as causes of cancer that any given employee can acquire from a work injury.

It is obvious that little wounds frequently repeated in the same place can be the cause of this terrible sickness. Yet, only one wound, even when this is a strong wound, is a decisive NO.

For this intelligent scientific conclusion, what was taken into account were the bullet wounds that were produced during the First World War of 1914-1918.

Is cancer produced by a germ? Official science affirms no, it is not. They emphasise the concept that this frightful sickness is not caused by any type of microbe or germ.

Revolutionary, scientific Gnosticism permits itself, with all respect, the liberty of disagreement. We, the Gnostics, affirm the existence of the "cancro," the microbe or germ of cancer.

Is cancer transmittable? It is obvious that the official science, after many experiments, answers with a categorical NO.

Nevertheless, exceptions exist, for example: cancer was inoculated into a rat which was nourished with a diet poor in copper and low in catalase. The result was positive: the rat became infected. It is indubitable that when this experiment has been repeated, the same results have been obtained.

In an opposite experiment, cancer was inoculated into a rat which had been previously prepared with a diet very rich in copper and catalase. The result was negative: the rat was not infected.

Official science has discovered that hydrogen peroxide, "oxygenated water," particularly increases the catalase and protects against the undesirable development of cancer.

We understand that the germ of cancer, the terrible "cancro," is developed in organisms that are poor in copper and catalase.

It is unquestionable that the "cancro" cannot be seen, not even through the most potent electron microscopes. However, if this dreadful sickness can be transmitted to organisms which are poor in copper and catalase, then it is obvious that such a microbe exists.

The germ of cancer develops and unfolds within the fourth dimension. It only allows itself to be observed in the tri-dimensional world through its destructive effects.

It is indubitable that in the future the most powerful electron microscope will be invented. Then, the "cancro" will be perceptible for the ultra-modern scientists.

It is obvious that this fatal germ arrives to the planet Earth submerged within the electromagnetic currents from the constellation of Cancer.

By all means, cancer is the karma of fornication. It is obvious that ancient wise men knew in depth this very special type of Nemesis.

Here in Mexico, a very special plant exists that can cure cancer. I want to emphatically refer to a certain bush-plant which is known in the region of Ixmiquilpan, state of Idalgo. The name of this bush-plant is "aranto." Ancient aboriginal people baptized this plant with the indigenous name of "aulaga."

The complete data, which is delivered by our beloved Gnostic brother Alfonso Silva, is very interesting.

"Mr. Mario Aponte, chief of the office of the former Electric Force and Light Company from the Mexican Republic, Misquiahuala, Idalgo, was attacked by a sickness in his gums. It is obvious that he did not acknowledge it.

"He then travelled to Mexico City with the good purpose of consulting the physicians from the electricians union. They diagnosed him with cancer of the mouth.

"Unsatisfied with such a diagnosis, the mentioned gentleman consulted other doctors. However, the diagnosis given by all of them was the same.

"Mr. Aponte returned to Misquiahuala very afflicted. Obviously, he could not remain absent from his office for a long time.

"This cited gentleman narrated that a little old lady from that place made the agreement of healing him with a vegetal tea, which she, herself, would give him to drink in his presence. This was because she feared the patient would not drink the remedy by himself.

"The results were extraordinary. In a period of eight months, Mr. Aponte was radically cured.

AULAGA

"He continued drinking the tea of this old lady. It was not necessary for her to give him the tea or to beg him to drink it, because the cited man was asking for it daily.

"One month later, the doctors from Mexico City, with astonishment, had to acknowledge that the cancer had disappeared."

The Gnostic brother Alfonso Silva continued by saying:

"To this date, from the people who I had offered the 'aranto' or 'aulaga,' I remember the name of Mrs. Luisa Lara de Barroeta, who is my sister-in-law. She was close to being operated on within the Social Security Institute for a cancerous tumor. It was the type of tumor in the womb, something very grave.

"This sick woman became radically healed by drinking infusions of 'aranto' and until this date she lives totally cured.

Thus, our Frater Silva continues by telling us:

"Mr. Agustin Uribe's spouse (we do not wish to reveal her address) was prepared by the physicians with the purpose of extracting a tumor from her liver. Yet, when they evidenced that this was a cancerous tumour, they immediately stitched her up at once, obviously declaring her a lost case. There was no chance for her, since the doctors found her abdominal cavity filled with cancerous tumors.

"However, this sick woman was definitively healed with the 'aranto' and still lives, thanks to the astonishing virtues of this bush-plant."

The distinguished physician, Doctor of Medicine Jacinto Juarez Parra from the National University of Mexico, tested the power of this bush-plant on a cancerous, terminally ill woman, already without hope. In this case, indeed, it was very difficult and it was not possible to save the life of this sick woman. I think that when the organism is already totally destroyed because of this sickness, every remedy fails.

Dr. Juarez considers that research with the electron microscope can and must be performed on this whole plant. By centrifugation, the nucleus, the lysosomes, the ribosomes and the microsomes must be separated in order to make a spectro-photometric analysis of each one of the parts of this plant. This would be for the intelligent purpose of discovering its colloids, enzymes, and its print element or oligo element. It must be investigated, says Dr. Juarez, to see which intracellular portions of this cited plant effectively act over the cancer.

The mentioned physician continues saying that every cancerous patient who is diagnosed through stimulating cytology and biopsy, will be medicated with the "aranto," as well as dosages of catalase and copper, and later he will again make another measurement with the diagnostic data.

Catalase and copper are low in cancerous people, and this is already completely demonstrated.

It is necessary to investigate the amount of sanguineous catalase and the dosage of copper in the plasma.

Any organism poor in catalase and copper is a proper field for the complete development of the dreadful "cancro."

A PAGE FROM THE BOOK OF THE DEAD

O Ra, verily, the Divine Eye of Horus liveth,
yea liveth within the Sanctuary of the great
temple, the Divine Eye of Horus liveth, yea
liveth, and its esoteric name is An-Maaut-f.

Chapter 39

The Triple Dominion of Seth

Lo and behold, that the white shining Eye of Horus cometh. The brilliant Eye of Horus as a mystic look-out cometh. It harmoniously cometh in peace, it sendeth forth rays of light as Ra (the intimate Logoi) in the horizon, and (thanks to meditation and with the help of the sacred snake) it destroyeth the triple power of Seth (the ego) according to the decree.

It leadeth him on, and it taketh possession of him (towards the Infernal Worlds) and the flames of this Divine Eye are kindled against him.

May I bring adoration unto its regenerator flame (my divine Mother Kundalini) that cometh and goeth about (she has the power of eliminating all of those perverse entities or screaming quarrelsome "I's" that constitute the ego).

It cometh and goeth about heaven encircling Ra (the intimate Logoi) and maketh him reign upon the divine ordering...!

O Ra, verily, the Divine Eye of Horus liveth, yea liveth within the Sanctuary of the great temple, the Divine Eye of Horus liveth, yea liveth, and its esoteric name is An-Maaut-f. - The Book of the Dead

It is unquestionable that the multiple tenebrous entities which personify our psychological defects constitute the ego (Seth). Therefore, the triple power of Seth is clear, obvious, and manifest. It is obvious that the red demons ("I's" or tenebrous entities) of Seth, express themselves through our body of desires (Judas), through our mental animal vehicle (Pilate) and through our bestial will (Caiaphas).

We already stated in former chapters and now we repeat in this one again that the intellectual animals mistakenly called human beings still do not possess the authentic Astral, Mental, and Causal vehicles.

It is very painful to have to emphatically affirm that instead of these mentioned solar vehicles, these wretched rational homunculi, indeed, only have three perverse demons within. These are the three wicked friends of Job.

It is obvious that this perverse race of Adam is one hundred percent diabolic. It is unquestionable that these wretched people do not have their Being incarnated. My words might seem severe to many readers; however, we must not hide the truth...

How difficult it is to build the glorious bodies of Kam-ur...! These Christic vehicles can only be created in the flaming forge of Vulcan...

The Nativity of the heart, the incarnation of the Being within ourselves, is only possible if we dress ourselves with the garments of Osiris (the Solar Bodies).

Nonetheless, I tell you: woe unto those who after having reached the Second Birth continue alive...!

Those ones, oh God! will convert themselves as a fact into Hanasmussen (abortions of the divine Mother Kundalini) with a double center of gravity.

It is obvious that the Being dressed with the Wedding Garment of the Soul (To Soma Heliakon) constitutes in Himself an ineffable and terrifically divine solar entity...

It is obvious that Seth, dressed with the triple tenebrous aspect of the lunar bodies, assumes the undesirable form of a lunar, abominable black magician...

For instance: when one invokes the Hanasmuss Andramelek, then either the white Master or the black Master can concur to the invocation. Nevertheless, both personages are the same individual.

Therefore, after the Second Birth, which the great Kabir Jesus talked about unto the great Rabbi Nicodemus, one finds oneself between two paths: the right hand path and the sinister path... It is evident, clear, and manifest that the left-hand path is the path of the Hanasmussen (this word is plural. The singular pronunciation is Hanasmuss).

This order of concomitances invites us to think in the inevitable urgency for a radical and definitive moral asepsis from the very beginning.

Such intimate asepsis is achieved by reducing into cosmic dust all of those red devils or tenebrous "I's" that express themselves within ourselves through the three wicked friends of Job...

As a sequence, we can emphasise the irrefutable idea that to intend the radical elimination of the three traitors of Hiram Abiff, without the previous death of the pluralized "I" (Seth), would be an absurdity...

Indeed and by all means it is easy to understand that each psychological defect is found personified in some tenebrous form...

Buddha taught that the ego is constituted by a sum of psychological aggregates (devil "I's").

Such aggregates are perishable. The unique thing that within ourselves assumes transcendental aspects of everlastingness is our Innermost Buddha. Unfortunately, this wretched humanity does not have Him incarnated.

This secret Buddha is so distinct from our body, our mind, and our most intimate affections, as oil is to water, as day is to night, as winter is to summer...

It is frightful to know that the secret Buddha is the judge of ourselves, of our own affections, sentiments, thoughts, desires, loves, passions... etc., etc., etc...

That my Being is the judge of myself?... This is terrible, yet it is true...

Therefore, by no means does my interior Buddha want me to exist... He wants my radical death...

How beautiful it is to die from moment to moment...! What is new arrives only with death...!

The secret Buddha becomes our best friend only after the death of Seth (the ego)...

The reason for the Being to be is to be the Being himself...

THE CENTER OF THE WHEEL OF SAMSARA

Seth, the pluralized "I," does not reincarnate.
Seth, the pluralized "I," only comes back,
returns, or re-incorporates himself within new
physical organisms, that is all.

Chapter 40

Return and Reincarnation

Behold, I am here in Parral in front of the grave of the General Pancho Villa. I call with a great voice, I invoke, I beckon...

The sails palpitate, shaken by the nocturnal breeze, as the wings of birds in flight, and the air upon the face of the gusting whirl minutely wrinkles the blue silk, a silken yarn of crystal stamens.

Then, someone terrible from within the profundity of the black sepulchre answers. It is the phantom of the noble general...

He upbraids me with severe words... His ex-personality gets up, he recognizes me, because I was also in the Division of the North. I enrolled with my people in his army.

Then, I exclaim, "Go back now into your sepulchre!" Thus, that shadow returned into the sepulchral fossa...

Later on, I visited some other pantheons. I invoked my ancient comrades of battle. Thus, they came unto my call, dispersing races and trampling upon centuries...

Amazingly, the laws of time were girding each soul to its tomb, who with a lugubrious howling was shouting, "Here I am...!"

Thus, oh God of mine...! From within every sepulchre was emerging, as by dint of magic, some of my comrades who died on the field of battle...

All of them recognized me... I conversed with all of them. Then after, each one of them returned into his sepulchral fossa...!

After all of this, I remained meditative: what do the pseudo-esoterists know about this? What do the pseudo-occultists say about this theme?...

It is obvious that three things go into the sepulchre: the physical body, the vital depth of it, and the personality that slowly dissolves...

It is unquestionable that not all goes into the sepulchre. There is something that continues beyond. I am referring to Seth, the ego, the myself.

By no means do we exaggerate if we emphasise the correct idea that what survives is a bunch of devils ("I"s)...

It is obvious that a psychic Essence exists within ourselves. Unfortunately, it is bottled up within all of those devil "I"s.

Such devil "I"s commonly concur to the spiritualist centers. They then penetrate into the bodies of the mediums and identify themselves.

The world gains nothing with those mediumistic, tenebrous experiments. The karma for such mediumistic people is epilepsy in their subsequent lives...

Seth, the pluralized "I," does not reincarnate. Seth, the pluralized "I," only comes back, returns, or re-incorporates himself within new physical organisms, that is all.

The word "reincarnation" is very demanding. The doctrine of Krishna teaches that only the Gods, Devas, Divine Kings, Demi-Gods, etc., etc. reincarnate. Unfortunately, in the western world, this term has been abundantly abused...

In ancient times, in Tibet, the reincarnations were celebrated with great festivities...

We need to die from moment to moment if indeed what we want is to individualize ourselves...

The pluralized "I" excludes any type of individuality...

By no means can individuality exist where there is the coexistence of multiple entities ("I"s), who quarrel amongst themselves and who originate within ourselves various psychological contradictions...

Therefore, reincarnation is only for sacred individuals...

When Seth dies in an integral way, then only the Being remains within ourselves. The Being is the one who gives us authentic individuality...

When Seth is disintegrated in a total way, then the consciousness, the Soul, is liberated and becomes radically awakened. Thus, the interior illumination arrives...

It is obvious that much later, we must attain the Upper-Individuality, if indeed what we aspire to is the Final Liberation.

In proportion, as we elevate ourselves throughout the marvellous gradation of this complete revolutionary development, we then become completely aware of the fact that in the previous levels that we were working in, we almost always committed the mistake of confounding the shadows with the realities.

When we have achieved the Final Liberation, throughout many deaths and renunciations, each time more and more terrific, then, any Mayavic Veil will cease to exist for ourselves.

Nevertheless, upon the face of the earth
there still exist some Mahatmas who can
study the memories of Nature within the
records of the omnipresent Okidanokh.

Chapter 41
The Akashic Records

Any deductive or inductive logical system invites us to comprehend that the whole history of the Earth and of its Root Races could not have been lost.

The Hindu sages frequently state in their books to us about that which we can indeed denominate Akash, the *causa causorum* of the Ether of science...

This Akashic substance is the same omnipresent and omni-penetrating Okidanokh, which fills the whole infinite space...

All of the cosmic concentrations from the infinite space are the mathematical outcome of the multiple crystallizations of the omnipresent Okidanokh...

It is written within old archaic documents that when the human beings were still in possession of that sight which is called "Olooesteskhniana vision" (the open Eye of Dangma), then they could correctly perceive all of the cosmic concentrations from starry space.

Hence, the human beings knew how to read the Akashic records of Nature. In those forgone times, nobody ignored the memories of creation.

However, when the human beings abused sex, when they ate from the tree of the science of good and evil, their terrestrial visual organ progressively degenerated, thus converting them into that which is called a common and current "Koritesnokhniano," one who has eyes that only see the tri-dimensional world of Euclid.

Nevertheless, upon the face of the earth there still exist some Mahatmas who can study the memories of Nature within the records of the omnipresent Okidanokh.

Any event leaves its living photograph within the Akash. It is obvious that all of our former lives are within those mysterious cosmic records.

Electronics is advancing marvellously in these modern times, thus, what we need now is a special device in order to capture the vibratory waves from the past.

When such a device is invented, then we will see and hear on the televised screen the whole history of the uncountable centuries.

This is how the Akashic records will inexorably fall into the hands of the scientists.

It has been stated unto us that the F.B.I. of the U.S.A. presently possesses a very special photographic camera, with which they can register on very sensible films homicides which were perpetuated many hours or days before they were announced to the authorities. In other words, it is inferred that if the agents of the law arrived at the place of the crime, they can photograph said crime with such a camera, even if this has been committed many hours or days before. Such revolutionary cameras work with infrared rays and an absolute void. We have been informed that the cooling process of its extremely fine lenses reaches the temperature of 15 to 20 degrees below zero.

This signifies that the Akashic records of Nature are now beginning to fall into the hands of modern sages.

It is obvious that if photographs related with past events are now being taken, then in a little while movies of this type could be filmed.

This is how in this New Aquarian Age, the men of science will have to recognize the esoteric and occultist affirmations.

Chapter 42
Lucifer

We have arrived in this present 1969-1970 Christmas Message to a very thorny problem. I am emphatically referring to Lucifer-Venus, unto whom Isaiah (14:12) offered that ineffable chant of pure mysticism, as follows:

> *How art thou fallen from heaven, O shining star, son of the morning, thou who looketh so brilliant at dawning?*

How can we indeed comprehend the profound mystery of the rebellion in heaven if we do not rend the veil which covers the Luciferian mysteries?

Let us remember the seven "children of inertia" from the Egyptian Mysteries who were thrown out from Am-smen, or paradise.

Let us not forget, beloved reader, the seven kings of the Babylonian legend of creation, the seven monarchs of the book of Revelation, the seven chroniclers or vigilantes from heaven, stars who disobeyed the commands of God, therefore they were tossed out of heaven.

So, what can we say about the seven constellations that the Book of Enoch refers to? Oh, God of mine...! These ones were lain aside as the seven refulgent mountains upon which the scarlet dame is seated...

It is written in the Akashic records of Nature that a third of the resplendent host, who are named Dhyanis or Arupa, frightfully fell into animal generation...

The degradation of Gods into demons is not an exclusive myth of Christianity, likewise, this has occurred with Zoroastrianism and Brahmanism and even with Chaldaean esoterism...

That the Angels of Light, Asuras, or Ahuras, breaths or blowing of the supreme Spirit, became demons...? Why should this be doubted? Is this perhaps a rare thing?

Any sacred individual can convert himself into a demon if he falls into animal generation...

It is unquestionable that the three traitors (Judas, Pilate, and Caiaphas) are reborn inside any sacred individual when such a one falls into bestial generation.

It is pathetic, clear, and manifest that the pluralized "I" (Seth) can resurrect like the Phoenix bird from within its own ashes...

Therefore, the theogonies are not mistaken when depicting those divine Logoi as punished for having committed the error of falling into sexual generation after the separation of the Lemurian Root Race into opposite sexes...

That they sacrificed themselves as Prometheus in order to endow the human being of that primeval infantile paradise with a conscious spirit? Mendacity! Ignorance! Absurdity!

I was a spectator and actor at the same time of the Genesis of life. Therefore, in the name of truth, I tell you that there was not such a sacrifice... We, the Lemurians, enjoyed sexual copulation; we fell into bestial generation because of pleasure!

It is obvious that this unusual and unexpected affirmation will cause a sound note of amazement onto many readers...

However, if the readers know of the doctrine of Reincarnation, then they should not become amazed...

That a human being was reincarnated in Lemuria? That he remembers his past lives? That he can give an archaic testimony? Well, this is normal; this is neither something rare nor strange...

Let us now go a little bit deeper: Gods and Devas, ineffable Pitris and Demi-Gods, were reincarnated in Lemuria.

That those divine Logoi, that those rebel Angels endowed this wretched intellectual homunculi, mistakenly called human beings, with a mental body? It is false, a lie...!

The wretched rational animal, instead of receiving as inheritance the authentic mental body, the unique thing that he received was Pilate, the demon Hai of the Egyptian mysteries.

The rational animal has not incarnated his Spirit because he has not yet built his Solar Bodies in the forge of the Cyclops.

The wretched tri-brained or tri-centred biped, erroneously qualified as human, is unconscious and ignorant.

In the name of truth and at any cost, I see myself in the necessity of affirming that I also was a fallen Archangel. Therefore, I have complete cognition of what I am writing in this message. I am not repeating somebody's theories; I affirm what I know.

I repented of my errors, I rose up from the mud of the earth. Now I give testimony of these things.

This wretched humanity gained nothing with the rebellion of the Angels of heaven. It would have been better to have known how to obey the Father.

The pseudo-esoterists and pseudo-occultists could object that after the human division into opposite sexes, sexual co-operation for the reproduction of the species was indispensable. This objection is not valuable for the Gods. It is unquestionable that the Men-Gods from Lemuria could have preserved their physical bodies throughout millions of years by means of the Elixir of Longevity of the Alchemists...

The following is for the acknowledgement of our readers: in some secret places of the world, immortal Lemurians still live.

My Holy Guru, whose sacred name I must not mention, still preserves the same physical body that he had in Lemuria.

It is obvious that I, particularly after the downfall in Lemuria, repented myself and returned into the mysteries of that ancient continent. Then, I received the Elixir of Long Life.

In the name of that which is the Reality, the TAO, the Divine, I tell you that I lived with an immortal physical body for millions of years...

Disobedience was not indispensable for the multiplication of the human species.

It is obvious that such a rebellion was an insentient action. The Men-Angels of the continent Mu could have donated their physical vehicles to the souls of the earth who were coming from the superior animal kingdoms without the necessity of violating the law.

THE EXPULSION FROM EDEN. ENGRAVING BY GUSTAVE DORÉ

*He that is of God heareth God's words: ye therefore
hear them not, because ye are not of God.*

It is unquestionable that all the people who live upon the face of the earth are children of Adam and Eve, the original couple, the Lemurian Root Race, who fell in the Luciferian sin of lust.

It is indubitable that the wretched people continue in the original Luciferian sexual sin.

We are children of lust and we continue with lust. This is obvious; it stands out to the naked eye.

That which is divine cannot be lustful. Therefore, we are not children of God, but of the devil.

Let us remember the words of Christ when he stated:

> I speak that which I have seen with my Father: and ye do that which ye have seen with your father.

> They answered and said unto him, Abraham is our father. Jesus saith unto them, If ye were Abraham's children, ye would do the works of Abraham.

> But now ye seek to kill me, a man that hath told you the truth, which I have heard of God: this did not Abraham.

> Ye do the deeds of your father. Then said they to him, We be not born of fornication; we have one Father, even God.

> Jesus said unto them, If God were your Father, ye would love me: for I proceeded forth and came from God; neither came I of myself, but he sent me.

> Why do ye not understand my speech? even because ye cannot hear my word.

> Ye are of your father the devil, and the lusts of your father ye will do. He was a murderer from the beginning, and abode not in the truth, because there is no truth in him. When he speaketh a lie, he speaketh of his own: for he is a liar, and the father of it.

> And because I tell you the truth, ye believe me not.

> Which of you convinceth me of sin? And if I say the truth, why do ye not believe me?

> He that is of God heareth God's words: ye therefore hear them not, because ye are not of God. - John 8:38-46

Two basic fires exist within the human being and within Nature.

The first is the fire of Maha-Kundalini.

The second is the fire of Lucifer-Venus.

It is obvious that the first is a divine fire. It is unquestionable that the second is a diabolic, passional, lustful fire.

Much has been stated about Agni - the God of Fire, Duksha - the Universal Father of every force. Evidently, knowledge, as the supreme force for Zoroastrians, magicians, and alchemists, is the beginning of all forces.

It is evident that we must search for such a supreme force within the central sun, which without any doubt is the most elevated among the four celestial suns. The last one among them is our physical sun, which is the original fountain of the sidereal light or astral light of Paracelsus and the Hermetic ones. If physically this force is the Ether, in its more sublime spiritual sense that is related with the Anima Mundi, it is the origin of the stars that are Christic granulated fire.

By confronting fires, inquiring, investigating, we discover with astonishment a notable igneous antithesis of a submerged lunar type...

I want to refer to Lucifer, the tempting serpent of Eden, that fatal fohatic force that when developed within the human being converts itself, as a fact and by its own right, into the abominable Kundabuffer organ (the tail of Satan).

We can infer with all of this without the fear of being mistaken that Seth (the pluralized "I"), as well as the three wicked friends of Job, are vile granulations of the lunar Luciferian fire within the atomic infernos of the human being.

It is obvious that the original human couple (the Lemurian Root Race) was the fatal sexual victim of the Luciferian serpent.

The rebellion in heaven and the consequent downfall of Angels is one hundred percent a sexual problem...

Lucifer, that vile worm who passes through the heart of the world, abides, as it is natural, in the depth of any organic or inorganic matter.

This lunar Luciferian fohat exercises direct control upon a certain malignant atom in the coccyx, sexual organs, heart, and brain.

This malignant Luciferian sexual impulse controls even our most intimate feelings.

Is indubitable that this blind fohatic force of a Luciferian lunar type has hypnotized the whole humanity, submerged it into the unconsciousness.

It is easy to comprehend that when this Luciferian Fire crystallizes in the entire legion of devil "I's" that every one carries inside, the outcome is the unconsciousness.

It is obvious that our consciousness sleeps within all of those tenebrous entities that constitute the ego.

This is how the Luciferian hypnotic process is developed inside each subject who lives upon the face of the earth.

The intellectual animal mistakenly called human being is ninety-nine percent Luciferian.

If it was not for the psychic essence that is bottled up within the ego, then the rational homunculi would be one hundred percent Luciferian.

Therefore, we must start from zero and recognize that we are demons, if indeed what we want is to reach the inner Self-realization of the Being.

First of all, we must eliminate the secret Pharisee from our interior nature. Let us remember the words of Jesus:

> But woe unto you, scribes and Pharisees, hypocrites! for ye shut up the kingdom of heaven (with all of those theories which you have) against men: for ye neither go in yourselves, neither suffer ye them that are entering to go in. - Matthew 23:13
>
> Ye blind guides (who are not illuminated) which strain at a gnat, and swallow a camel.

Woe unto you scribes and Pharisees, hypocrites! for ye make clean the outside of the cup and of the platter, but within they are full extortion and excess. - Matthew 23:24-25

Woe unto you scribes and Pharisees, hypocrites! (fanatic puritans who commit crimes and thereafter wash their hands) for ye are like unto whited sepulchres, which indeed appear beautiful outward (filled with fake humbleness and with sublime pietistic postures), but are within full of dead men's bones, and of all uncleanness.

Even so ye also outwardly appear righteous unto men (and you even self-cheat yourselves by believing yourselves to be good and holy), but within (even if you will never believe it, indeed,) ye are full of hypocrisy and iniquity. - Matthew 23:27-28

The Master 'G' commits the mistake of confounding the Kundalini with the Luciferian fire of the abominable Kundabuffer organ. He (Master 'G') even grants unto the Kundalini all of the sinister aspects of the Kundabuffer.

It is obvious that we need to comprehend and to eliminate. This is already stated in previous chapters.

It is obvious that the Kundalini, the igneous serpent of our magical powers, is a terribly divine Vedantic and Jehovistic truth.

The ascending fire of Kundalini victoriously opens, within the dorsal spine of the human being, the seven seals of the Apocalypse of Saint John.

Devi Kundalini, our divine adorable Mother, is the ascending serpent of the spinal medullar canal...

She, the divine snake, has the power to eliminate the red demons of Seth.

The sacred viper can destroy the crystallizations or granulations of the Luciferian serpent.

Therefore, we are before the two serpents.

The first one victoriously ascends throughout the spinal canal of the human organism.

The second one descends; it precipitates itself from the coccyx downwards towards the atomic infernos of the human being.

The first one is the Serpent of Bronze that healed the Israelites in the wilderness.

The second one is the tempting serpent of Eden, Lucifer, the horrible Python snake that is writhing in the mud of the earth and that Apollo enragedly hurts with his darts.

Very interesting reminiscences come into my memory in these moments... One certain delectable night, it does not matter which one, while being in that Zen state known as Satori or Samadhi (ecstasy), I joyfully entered through the doors of the temple upon the wings of longing.

Thus, as many other seated adepts, I also sat and listened to the delectable chants...

What those golden voices uttered profoundly touched even the most intimate fibers of my soul...

All of us were then praising the Emperor, that Divine Monad of every one, who before the dawning of the Mahamanvantara was moving upon the chaotic waters of the infinite space...

The spiral, snailshell-shaped stairs conduced upwards to the high floor of the temple.

It is obvious that such a spiral ladder ended exactly at the foot of the sacred altar of the Emperor.

The sacrarium was gloriously shining upon the most sacred altar, and the fire was burning within its lamp...

Some flower pots were marvellously completing such a precious enchantment...

It is obvious that the flowers always endow a certain exquisite something, wherever they are...

Nonetheless, there was something more, something unusual, a strange set of figures skilfully carved in wood...

Such figures were exactly placed in front of the altar, upon that mysterious, divine ladder. It represented, as a fact, a serious inconvenience, a tremendous obstacle in order to arrive in front of the interior Lord...

I, then in fight against the third traitor of Hiram Abiff, had to profoundly study the symbolism of those hieratic figures of mystery...

They were a variegated and painteresque conjunction of strange wooden beings upon the polished steps of the holy ladder...

To concentrate my attention upon such artistic representations was indispensable...

The royal art of Nature is nothing dead: it has life, abundant life...

Let us remember those living pictures seen by Franz Hartmann inside the Gnostic Rosicrucian Temple of Bohemia, Germany.

Hartmann, when concentrating his attention upon a Tibetan representation, could see a Mahatma who was riding his vigorous stallion. The Mahatma saluted him from afar, and while smiling, he rode away...

This is what the royal art from the White Brotherhood is: something which has life, something precious.

Therefore, the attentive reader should by no means be surprised if I tell him that when I concentrated my attention upon such very finely carved exotic figures, they came to life...

Even if this seems incredible, since everything is possible in the unknown dimension, when seeing them, I beheld something unusual...

In a certainly unexpected way, one of those figures suddenly freed itself. It had the appearance of an Elder dressed in an exotic way. The voice of the silence informed me that it was related with the Lord of time. I was instructed that I must eliminate the useless refuse of the past...

I understood everything. Thus, the Elder walked holding in his dexterous hand a strange container filled with garbage...

I comprehended in depth the deep significance of such an allegory. The filthy reminiscences of the past, the garbage of many yesterdays, must be forgotten...

The Elder dug a sepulchral fossa in the pantheon of the dead. Then, he buried the useless debris there...

It is unquestionable that thereafter, when his symbolic labor was accomplished, the Elder returned to his place...

Afterwards, another figure detached itself from that strange set. I was instructed that it was Lucifer, who works in time. It was indicated to me that Lucifer achieves the resurrection of the dead "I's" by means of memories...

Thus, I saw Lucifer walking among the sepulchres of time. He searches for the buried "I's" within the dust of the centuries; he wants to turn them to life again. I contemplated him in absorption...

How sly Lucifer is! He awakens lustful, sinful memories within oneself, so that the dead "I's" can resurrect...

Then, I comprehended in depth the necessity of living from instant to instant, from moment to moment...

Alas, oh God of mine! The "I" is time. Yes! Yes! Yes...! However, the Being is non-temporal. He is that which is always new...

Once this other illustration finished, the Luciferian figure returned to his mysterious place...

Then, I concentrated my attention in a most intense way. Thus, I saw something that stood out: it was a fatal flame. It was clear that such a sinister fire assumes a terrible, masculine form. The voice of the silence told me that Lucifer controls the three traitors of Hiram Abiff and the remnants of the ego after his final disintegration. This is how I did understand it. So, I approached Lucifer and I told him that I was his friend. He then laughed at me, and by talking he addressed me and made me to understand that I was his enemy. It is obvious that this diabolic fire did not make a mistake concerning his remarks...

Incredible! Even after the "I" has died, Lucifer continues controlling even the seeds of the ego... What a horror...!

Remember, dear reader, that the "I" can also resurrect as the Phoenix bird from within its own ashes.

Therefore, the rebellion in the heavens was a very complex process of the resurrection of the ego and of the three wicked friends of Job within each sacred individual.

It is obvious that the Luciferian fire originated this special type of diabolical resurrection within the psyche of every Man-Angel of the continent Mu...

It is obvious that the Men-Angels, with the resurrection of the ego and the reviving of the three traitors, converted themselves into authentic demons...

In the preceding Mahamanvantara of Padma, or Lotus of Gold, these ineffable ones from this rebellion had already eliminated Seth and the three traitors. Unfortunately, Lucifer works in time...

It is unquestionable that the lunar Luciferian fire has the power of resuscitating Judas, Pilate, and Caiaphas. It is certain that Lucifer-Mara, the sexual tempter, can call to life all of those red demons from ancient times, all of those devil "I"s of Seth...

Chapter 43
Darkness

Ancient wisdom states that darkness is in itself Father-Mother, and light is its child.

It is evident that the uncreated light has an unknowable origin, which is absolutely unknowable to us...

In no way do we exaggerate if we emphasise the idea that the origin of the uncreated light is darkness.

The cosmos emerges from the chaos, and light sprouts from darkness. Let us profoundly pray..!

Let us now talk about the borrowed, secondary, cosmic light. It is obvious that whatever its origin might be, and whatever its beauty might be, it has in its depth a temporary "mayic" character...

Then, the profound, ineffable darkness constitutes the eternal womb, in which the origins of light appear and disappear...

It is unquestionable that in this, our afflicted world of samsara, nothing is added to the darkness in order to convert it into light.

It is clear that in this valley of bitterness, nothing is added to light in order to transform it into darkness.

The logic of thought, or better if we say the Tertium Organum, invites us to think that light and darkness are interchangeable.

Analyzing this from a rigorously scientific point of view, we arrive at the conclusion that light is only a mode of darkness, and vice versa.

Light and darkness are two phenomena of the same noumenon, which is unknowable, profound, and inconceivable to the reasoning...

The fact of perceiving more or less light that shines within the darkness is a matter that depends on our power of spiritual vision...

Brahma

Did you ever hear about Brahma? He is in
Himself Father-Mother-Son (Osiris, Isis, Horus)...

A great being stated, "What is light for us is darkness for certain insects, and the spiritual eye sees illumination where the normal eye can only see obscurity..."

After the Mahamanvantara, the universe immersed into a Pralaya, dissolved within its primordial element, necessarily reposed within the profound darkness of the infinite space...

It is urgent to deeply comprehend the profound mystery of the chaotic darkness.

It is written with characters of unmistakable fire in the book of the great life that at the end of the Mahamanvantara (Cosmic Day), Osiris (the Father), Isis (the Divine Mother Kundalini), and Horus (the Divine Spirit), are integrated, mixed, and fused like three fires, in order to make one single flame...

It is obvious and any Mahatma knows that during the Mahapralaya (Cosmic Night) the whole dissolved universe lies within the unique, eternal, and primary cause, in order to be reborn again in the following dawning of the new great Cosmic Day, as is periodically done by Karana, the eternal cause.

Let us search for Osiris, Isis, and Horus within ourselves, within the unknowable profundities of our own Being.

It is obvious that Osiris, Isis, and Horus constitute in themselves the Monad, the Duad, and the Triad of our Innermost Being...

Did you ever hear about Brahma? He is in Himself Father-Mother-Son (Osiris, Isis, Horus)...

In each new cosmic dawning, the universe resurrects, like the Phoenix bird from within its own ashes...

In the dawning of each Mahamanvantara, the Monad unfolds again into the Duad and into the Triad...

At the daybreak of the new Cosmic Day, after the profound Night, the Son, the Triad, Horus (the divine Spirit within each one of us), emanates the Essence, His mystic principles, from Himself into the Wheel of Samsara, with the purpose of acquiring a Diamond Soul...

Ah! How great the joy of Horus is when acquiring a Diamond Soul! Then, He is absorbed within His Divine Mother, and She is also fused with the Father, who together form a unique Diamond Flame, a God of resplendent, interior beauty...

Chapter 44
Substances, Atoms, Forces

The Master 'G,' when speaking about substances and forces, stated:

"Proceeding again with the law of three, we must learn how to find the manifestations of this law in everything we do and in everything we study.

"When this law is applied through any way or through any act, we will see that it reveals many new things to us, many things which formerly we did not see.

"Let us take chemistry for an example. Ordinary chemistry does not know of the Law of Trinity. Therefore, it studies the matter without taking into account its cosmic properties.

"However, another chemistry apart from the ordinary one exists. This is a special chemistry that we can call Alchemy, which is a chemistry that studies matter by taking into account its cosmic properties.

"As it was previously indicated, the cosmic properties of every substance are firstly determined by the place that this substance occupies and, secondly, by the force that acts through it in a given moment.

"Still, the nature of any given substance, though occupying the very same place, can suffer a great change. This change depends on the force that is manifesting itself through it.

"Each substance can be the conductor of the three forces (First, Second, and Third Logos). Thus, in accordance with this, the substance can be active, passive or neutral.

"In the case when none of the three forces manifest themselves through the substance at any given moment, or better, if the substance is taken without any relation to the manifestation of the three forces, then, the substance can neither be active, passive, nor neutral.

"Accordingly, the substance then appears in this way, in other words, in four aspects or different states.

"It is necessary, in this sense, to specifically take into account that when we refer to matter, we are not referring to chemical elements.

"This special chemistry that we are dealing with sees a separated function in each substance, even in the most complex substance. It sees the substance as an element.

"This is the only way in which the study of the cosmic properties of matter can be done, because all of the complex compounds have their own finality and cosmic purposes.

"If this question is seen from this point of view, then, we see that the atom of any given substance is nothing else than the most small quantity of such substance, which retains all of its chemical, physical and cosmic properties.

"Consequently, the size of the atoms in different substances is not always the same. Thus, in some cases, an atom could be a visible particle even to the physical eye.

"The four aspects or states of every substance have precise names.

"When a substance is the conductor of the first force or active force, it is called 'carbon'. Thus, it is designated with the letter 'C', as in the carbon of chemistry.

"When a substance is the conductor of the second force or passive force, it is called 'oxygen'. Hence, it is designated with the letter 'O', as in the oxygen of chemistry.

"When a substance is the conductor of the third force or neutral force, it is called 'nitrogen', and it is designated with the letter 'N', as in the nitrogen of chemistry.

"When the substance is taken without a relation with the force that manifests through it, it is called 'hydrogen'. Therefore, it is designated with the letter 'H', as in the hydrogen of chemistry.

"The active, passive and neutral forces are designed with the numbers 1, 2, 3, and the substances with the letters C, O, N, H. It is indispensable to understand these denominations.

"Petyr Ouspensky stated, 'One of us asked: Do these elements correspond to the four elements of Alchemy: fire, air, water, and earth?'

"'G' answered: 'Yes, effectively, they correspond to them. However, we will utilize these ones (C, O, N, H). Soon you will understand the reason why.'"

Well, here we finish with Master 'G's quotation. Now, let us go deeply into this Alchemical formulary...

We already stated in our former 1968-1969 Christmas Message about the Ain Soph or super divine Atom that abides within the unknowable profundities of our own Being...

In the final synthesis, each one of us is nothing more than an atom from the Abstract Absolute Space, which is the interior atomic star that has always smiled upon us.

A certain author has said: "I raise my eyes towards the utmost, towards the stars, from which, for me, all help has to come, but I always follow the inner star which guides my interior..."

We must make a specific differentiation between the Ain Soph and the Ain Soph Paranishpanna. In the Ain Soph, interior Self-realization does not exist, but in the Ain Soph Paranishpanna, realization of the Innermost Self does exist...

Any Mahatma knows very well that before entering into the Absolute, the Solar Bodies must be dissolved.

It is obvious that four atom-seeds remain from these Christic vehicles.

It is indubitable that such atom-seeds correspond to the physical, astral, mental, and causal bodies...

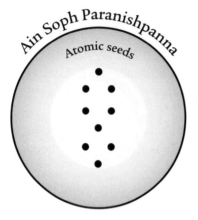

Atomic Seeds of the
Ain Soph Paranishpanna:

The Father
The Son
The Holy Spirit
Atman
The Divine Soul
Solar Causal Body
Solar Mental Body
Solar Astral Body
Physical Body

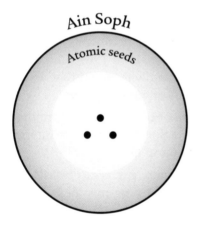

Atomic Seeds of the
Ain Soph:

The Father
The Son
The Holy Spirit

AIN SOPH AND AIN SOPH PARANISHPANNA

We must make a specific differentiation
between the Ain Soph and the Ain Soph
Paranishpanna. In the Ain Soph, interior
Self-realization does not exist, but in the
Ain Soph Paranishpanna, realization of the
Innermost Self does exist...

It is obvious that the four atom-seeds are absorbed within the super divine Atom, the Ain Soph Paranishpanna, along with the Essence, spiritual principles, laws, and the three primary forces... Afterwards, the profound night of the Mahapralaya arrives.

The Ain Soph without intimate Self-realization does not possess the four atom-seeds; it is just a simple atom of the Abstract Absolute Space. That is all.

In Alchemy, the letter 'C' symbolizes the Conscious Body of Willpower, it is the carbon of occult chemistry.

In Alchemy, the letter 'O' symbolizes the Solar Mental Body that was built in the forge of the Cyclops, the oxygen of sacred chemistry.

In Alchemy, the letter 'N' symbolizes the authentic Solar Astral Body, which is very different from the body of desires. It is obvious that the legitimate sidereal body is the nitrogen of occult chemistry.

In Alchemy, the 'H' symbolizes the physical body, the three-dimensional vehicle of flesh and bones.

We do not exaggerate if we emphasize the Alchemist's transcendental idea that an Ain Soph Paranishpanna atom possesses within itself the four atom seeds: carbon, oxygen, nitrogen, and hydrogen.

With these four Alchemical atoms, the Ain Soph Paranishpanna rebuilds the Mercabah, the chariot (the Solar Bodies), in order to enter into any universe when it is necessary...

Let us not forget that Mercabah is the chariot of the centuries, the heavenly human being of the Kabbalah...

As a sequence or corollary, we can, and we must affirm that those who have not performed the work in the Ninth Sphere (the sex) certainly do not possess the chariot, the Mercabah.

It is unquestionable that everything changes in the active field of the Prakriti, due to the modifications of the Trigunamayashakti, and that we, the human beings, also modify ourselves in a positive or negative way. But, if we do not build the chariot, the Mercabah, the Ain Soph remains without realization of the Innermost Self.

Those who have not eliminated the Abhayan Samskara, the innate fear, will flee from the Ninth Sphere by telling to others that the work in the forge of the Cyclops (sex) is worthless.

These are the hypocritical Pharisees who "strain at a gnat, and swallow a camel." These are the failed ones who "neither go into the Kingdom themselves, neither suffer they those who are entering to go in." Indeed, sex is a stumbling rock and a rock of offence...

Chapter 45
Pratimoksha

We start this chapter with a beautiful poem from Don Ramon del Valle Inclan:

Gnostic Rose

Nothing can be that has not formerly been.
Nothing can be that shall not become tomorrow.
Eternal all instants are and have been,
as the grain which the clock scrapes with sorrow.

Eternal is the rose's grace,
as the earliest skylark that announces the morning,
as the caterpillar, whose flower the butterfly did brace.
Eternal is, within my conscience, my guilt's mourning.

Reclined at the verge of the way, coated with rime,
is the worm which germinates in mud as swine,
this is how I sense the black anguish of my crime
as an aspiration to the whole divine.

The Gnostic mystery is present
in the quiet soaring of the dove
and the sin of the world in the (Tempting) serpent
which bites the foot of the angel who subdues it with love.

Upon the eternal nights of a forgone time
the eternal nights of tomorrow open, they grapple
each hour a larvae of crime
and the symbol of the serpent and the apple.

Time keeps the enigma of form,
as a dragon which keeps vigil upon the worlds
so that, the Whole and Unity, supreme norm,
can weave from its stele, the infinite worlds.

Nothing turns off the flame of the crucible,
for sealed in its bottom is, as eternal flaming rage,
the idea of Plato. Suns, distant and invisible
one day shall illuminate our hermitage.

While my shroud the Parca spins,
on my forehead, a cross of ashes, I represent.
Time is woodworm's dust, pains
through Satan. Yet, God is the present!

Everything is eternity! Everything happened already!
Thus everything which is now, shall be tomorrow
in these moments opened by this moment, making ready,
under our feet the hole of death, with sorrow!

Beautiful poem, is it not? "Nothing can be that has not
formerly been. Nothing can be that shall not become tomorrow."
Behold here the law of Recurrence. A constant repetition of
successive lives.

Thus, in every existence everything comes to occur again
such as it happened before. Indeed, "time is woodworm's dust,
pains through Satan..."

The repetition of this drama of existence is a vicious circle...

Do you want to know what will be your destiny in your future
existence? I want you to know that "upon the eternal nights of a
forgone time, the eternal nights of tomorrow open..."

Do you comprehend...? When again you will be born in this
valley of tears, the past will become future...

This signifies that your present life with all of its vain
happiness, sufferings, and sorrows will unfortunately be
repeated...

But, what about Epigenesis, or creation of new causes, then
what...? Woe, wretched mortals of the earth! Do you believe,
perchance, that the ego or pluralized "I" is capable of creating
something new...? Do you ignore that the ego is memory, that it
is accumulated dust from centuries...?

Gnostics...! It is indispensable for you to dissolve the ego.
To die from moment to moment is urgent. What is new arrives
only with death...!

Did you ever hear about the Buddhist Pratimoksha? This is
the ceremony of discharge. We, the Gnostics practice it...

To publicly confess our crimes, to exhibit them, to place
them over the carpet of actuality and not to hide them, signifies,
as a fact, to scorn oneself, to scorn one's "I."

One given night, I assisted with the Pratimoksha in the
Gnostic Church. Somebody else, it does not matter who, seated

himself upon a comfortable chair in front of the congregation and a great Being placed himself behind him.

The devotee publicly confessed all the crimes of his life in front of the Brotherhood...

After confessing some crime, the devotee paused. Then, in those moments, the priest and the congregation were begging to the penitent's Divine Mother Kundalini to cast the "I" that personified such a sin downwards into the Infernal Worlds...

It is obvious that the Divine Mother Kundalini wisely operated by eliminating the entity that personified the confessed crime.

I comprehended then that indeed, the Buddhist Pratimoksha is a ceremony of discharge.

To declare such crimes implied, as a fact, to publicly describe the history of his life.

It was explained to me that this type of Pratimoksha is practiced three or five times during the course of our existence.

Pertaining to the Gnostic Liturgy, a very special form of monthly Pratimoksha exists, which is very necessary for all the devotees. In this monthly Pratimoksha, the devotee publicly confesses in front of the fraternity only the crime or crimes committed within the last thirty days of his existence. (Study this, as it is explained in our Second Chamber book entitled *Gnostic Liturgy and Constitution for Gnostic Institutions*).

It is obvious that without the help of the Divine Mother Kundalini, the elimination of all the diverse entities that personify our errors would be impossible.

These diverse forms of Pratimoksha are very useful in order to eliminate all of those diverse psychological aggregates that constitute the ego.

The return of the seventy confirms the Pratimoksha:

> And the seventy returned again with joy saying, Lord, even the devils (egos of the people) are subject unto us through thy name.
> - Luke 10:17

It is written that Jesus, the great Kabir, answered:

> *I beheld Satan (the pluralized "I") as lightning fall from heaven. Behold I give unto you power to tread on serpents and scorpions (black entities of sin), and over all the power of the enemy, and nothing shall by any means hurt you.*
>
> *Notwithstanding, in this rejoice not, that the (malignant) spirits are subject unto you; but rather rejoice, because your names are written in heaven.* - Luke 10:18-20

Be careful, Gnostic priests, of falling into pride as a result of having been given the power in order to work with Devi Kundalini, for the elimination of the devil "I's"... Be meek, pure, and simple.

The Pratimoksha is necessary during the work with the gold and with the silver, with the Sun and with the Moon, in the forge of the Cyclops.

Let us remember Joshua uttering:

> *Sun stand thou still upon Gibeon; and thou Moon, in the valley of Ajalon.*
>
> *And the sun stood still, and the moon stayed (symbol of the esoteric work), until the people (the Initiates) had avenged themselves upon their enemies (their devil "I's").*
>
> *Is not this written in the book of Jasher? So the Sun (Christ) stood still in the midst of heaven (in order to guide the Initiate, as He always does it), and hasted not to go down about a whole day.* - Joshua 10:12-13

The Cosmic Christ, the Solar Logos, the Sun of midnight, guides all of those who fight against their enemies, the tenebrous "I's," the red devils of Seth, the ego.

Chapter 46
The Twelve Nidanas

Ancient wisdom emphasises the idea of seven "pathways" towards the ineffable joy of Non-existence, which is the Absolute Being and real Existence.

In its depth, such a luminous idea is unitary, since only one pathway with seven journeys exists.

Let us think of the astrological formula of the Moon, Mercury, Venus, Sun, Mars, Jupiter, and Saturn. It is unquestionable that each one of the seven worlds is intimately related with one of the seven journeys...

Did you ever hear about the twelve causes of the Being? What do you know about the Four Noble Truths?

It is obvious that the Twelve Nidanas and the Four Truths specially characterize the Hinayana system.

The Nidanas belong to that wise theory of the current of the concatenation law which produces merit and demerit and which finally manifests Karma in the whole plenitude of its power.

It is a system which has the famous laws of Transmigration, Return, and Recurrence as a foundation.

It is obvious that the Hinayana system - or Lesser Vehicle School - is of a very ancient origin, while the Mahayana or Greater Vehicle School belongs to a posterior period; it had its origin after the disincarnation of Buddha.

It is clear that in their depth, both schools teach the same esoteric doctrine. "Yana" or "vehicle" is a mystical expression. Therefore, both vehicles signify that we can escape from the torture of rebirths by means of the realization of the Innermost Self: the Being.

We need to dress with the Dharma-megha, the cloud of virtue, the marvellous splendor of the perfect ones who renounce powers.

All the diverse ideas that emerge and that make us believe that we need something exterior in order to be happy are obstacles for our perfection.

The Innermost Being is happiness and beatitude by His own nature. Unfortunately, knowledge of this is covered by past impressions.

It is urgent, it is indispensable, it is necessary, for such impressions to exhaust their effects.

Their destruction is done in the same manner as we do with ignorance and egotism, etc.

If when arriving at the correct discrimination of the essences, we even reject their fruition, then the Samadhi named Cloud of Virtue comes as a consequence.

Whosoever is dressed with the Cloud of Virtue is liberated from sufferings and works. Nevertheless, this does not signify that such a one is exempt from the possibility of downfall. We can pass beyond any danger only by entering into the Absolute.

The successive transformations of qualities only disappear when we absorb ourselves within the Abstract Absolute Space.

The changes that exist in relation with given moments and that are perceived at the end of a series of them become another succession of moments in the other extreme.

Succession does not exist for the Self-realized and Diamantine Spirit. Only the Eternal Present exists for Him. He lives from moment to moment. He has liberated Himself from the Twelve Nidanas.

Chapter 47
The Thymus Gland

The thymus is a very important gland of internal secretion and we must profoundly study it.

Men of science know very well that such a gland is found situated underneath the thyroid gland, in that forward superior mediastinal cavity (behind the upper thorax bones).

Any biologist knows by observation and direct experience that the thymus gland usually consists of two longitudinal lobes, united throughout a central plane.

The constitution of this marvellous and formidable gland is admirable. Each lobe is extraordinarily formed by even more small divisions that are called lobules.

It is obvious and any scientist can comprehend that each lobule is comprised of an external portion or cortex and a central portion or medulla.

It is obvious that the thymus gland of a child is relatively large. However, by all means it is clear to verify that during the last part of childhood, the weight of this gland gradually diminishes in relation to the weight of the body.

Biology teaches that the thymus gland marvellously evolves in children until acquiring a specific weight of 25 to 40 grams.

Endocrinologists do not ignore that such a gland generally starts its devolving processes between eleven and fourteen years of age. It is unquestionable that such a regression is very slow and it endures the whole life.

A wise author, whose name I do not mention, textually states the following:

> "We still do not know enough about the thymus gland; yet, it seems that this gland is the one that dominates the development of the child's body before puberty.

> "It inhibits the activity of the testicles and ovaries. Castration causes the persistent development of the thymus' body.

"The extraction of the thymus gland or its inhibition by means of x-rays accelerates the development of the gonads.

"The continued action of the thymus gland after puberty causes peculiarities in the sexual expression.

"Degenerated and repulsive practices appear invariably in the persons in whom the function of the thymus gland predominates.

"The thymus gland impedes the differentiation and stops the transformation towards a positive sexual expression, whether it is related with a man or a woman.

"If tadpoles are nourished with the thymus substance, then their development and differentiation into a male or female frog is impeded."

"People in whom the function of the thymus gland predominates become homosexual.

"The male does not entirely become male, and because within him remains too much that is potentially feminine, he likes the society of males more than the society of females.

"The female will still be potentially male and therefore she will enjoy more the company of the female.

"A multitude of criminal and degenerated persons are mainly people within whom the action of the thymus gland predominates.

"The thymus gland seems to be the conductor of the body of the creature. It furnishes it with many of the necessary elements for its structure.

"The thymus gland begins to hold its action during puberty. Therefore, it is supposed to be the propulsive gland for the infantile development.

"The process of calcification has become retarded in those animals in which the thymus gland has been extracted.

"It seems that the thymus gland dominates the lymphatic system."

Therefore, degenerated infrasexual people, like homosexuals and lesbians within whom lamentably the action of the thymus gland predominates, are the fatal outcome of a degenerated sexual seed.

It is obvious that a degenerated seed does not serve for the intimate Self-realization of the Being.

If the germ does not die, then the plant cannot be born. It is obvious that the real and true Human Being can only be born from the normal seed.

Homosexuality and lesbianism accuse, indicate, aim to a devolving, regressive, and descendent process.

It is pathetic, clear, and apparent that not a single legitimate school of regeneration would ever admit degenerated seeds inside of its bosom.

THE INITIATE IN THE HALL OF THE TWO TRUTHS

*Oh Gods! let not evil befall me in this land, and in your
Hall of Truth and Justice, because I, even I, know the
names of these gods who are therein and who are about
Maat, the great Divinity of Truth and Justice.*

Chapter 48
The Negative Confession I
(From the Papyrus of Nu)

Let us now utter from the profound depth of all ages. Listen to me, humans and Gods!

The negative confession from the Papyrus of Nu is for those human beings who have achieved radical and absolute death.

After the definitive annihilation of the ego and of the three traitors of Hiram Abiff, we can certainly give unto ourselves the luxury of penetrating into the double hall of the Truth and Justice, dressed with the glorious bodies of Kam-ur.

To intend to victoriously enter into the double hall of Maat without previously having passed through the supreme death would be useless... (We are not referring to the death of the physical body).

Only the authentic defuncts have the right to the negative confession. Indeed, only they can submit themselves to the terrible confession from the Papyrus of Nu of the Egyptian mysteries.

Let it be understood that the authentic defuncts are those who have died in themselves within the forty-nine regions of their subconsciousness.

Therefore, any true defunct can present himself, dressed with his Solar Bodies, in the double hall of Maat, in order to perform his Negative Confession.

Negative Confession

Homage to thee, Oh great God, thou Lord of Truth and Justice, I have come to thee, Oh powerful Lord.

I have brought myself hither that I may behold thy radiant beauty! I know thee and I know thy magic name and I know the names of the two and forty divinities who surround thee in this vast hall of Truth and Justice, who live as warders of sinners and who feed upon their blood on the day when the sins of men are taken into account in the presence of Osiris.

The two Goddesses, twin sisters with two eyes, Lord of the Order of the Universe is thy name.

Behold, that I have brought in my heart Truth and Justice to thee, since I have destroyed all wickedness from it, for thee.

I have not done evil to mankind. I have not oppressed the members of my family.

I have not brought injustice in the place of Justice. I have had no knowledge of worthless men. I have not wrought evil.

I have not made to be the first consideration of each day that excessive labor should be performed for me. I have not brought forward my name for exaltation to honours. I have not ill-treated servants. I have not thought scorn of Gods.

I have not defrauded the oppressed one of his property.

I have not done that which is an abomination unto the Gods. I have not caused harm to be done to the servant by his chief.

I have not caused pain. I have made no man to suffer hunger. I have made no one of my neighbors to weep.

I have done no murder. I have not given the order for murder to be done for me. I have not inflicted sicknesses upon mankind.

I have not defrauded the temples of their oblations. I have not purloined the cakes of the Gods.

I have not carried off the cakes offered to the sanctified spirits. I have not polluted myself by committing shameful actions within the sacrosanct precinct of the temples.

I have not diminished from the bushel. I have neither added to nor filched away land. I have not encroached upon the fields of others.

I have not added to the weights of the scales to cheat the seller. I have not mis-read the pointer of the scales to cheat the buyer. I have not carried away the milk from the mouth of children. I have not driven away the cattle which were upon their pastures.

I have not snared the feathered fowls of the preserves of the Gods. I have not caught fish with bait made of fish of their kind.

I have not turned back the water at the time when it should flow.

I have not cut a cutting in a canal of running water. I have not extinguished a fire or light when it should burn.

I have not violated the rules of the offerings, the chosen meat-offerings. I have not driven off the cattle from the property of the temples of the Gods.

I have not repulsed a God in his manifestation. I am pure! I am pure! I am pure!

My purity is the purity of that great Phoenix which is in the city of Heracleopolis.

For, behold, I am the Lord of the respiration who maketh all the Initiates to live on the solemn day when the Eye of Horus in the presence of the Divine Lord of this earth which is Heliopolis at the end.

For behold, I have seen the Eye of Horus in Heliopolis at the end, therefore, Oh Gods! let not evil befall me in this land, and in your Hall of Truth and Justice, because I, even I, know the names of these gods who are therein and who are about Maat, the great Divinity of Truth and Justice.

Here ends the Negative Confession from the Papyrus of Nu. In our future 1970-1971 Christmas Message, we will continue with the Papyrus II (Nebsenti).

ZEN

Chapter 49

Koan

What is a Koan exercise? This is something that we, the Gnostics, must profoundly study.

Koan is the Japanese pronunciation of the Chinese phrase Kung-an, whose original meaning is, "Document of an official agreement on the desk."

It is obvious that Zen Buddhists give the term Koan a totally different meaning.

It is obvious that they designate as Koan a certain mystical dialogue between Master and disciple.

For example: A certain monk asked the Master Tung Shan, "Who is the Buddha?" The Master strangely answered, "Three chin (a measurement) of flax."

A Buddhist monk asked the Master Chao Chou, "What is the meaning of the arrival of the Bodhisattva from the west?" The answer was, "The cypress tree that is in the garden."

An enigmatic answer, is it not? All these famous stories that are narrated in the aforementioned manner are Koans.

It is evident, clear, and obvious that Koan designates a Zen story, a Zen situation, a Zen problem.

The esoteric Koan exercise generally means, "To seek the solution to a Zen problem."

Behold here some Koan examples for meditation:

"Who recites the name of Buddha?"

"If all things are reduced to the Unity, what can the Unity be reduced to?"

It is unquestionable that the mind will never be able to solve a Zen problem. It is obvious that our understanding will never be able to comprehend the deep significance of a Koan.

By all means it is easy to foresee that when the mind tries to integrally comprehend any Koan, it fails and becomes defeated. Then, the mind remains in a profound stillness and in silence.

Thus, when the mind is still, when the mind is in silence, the new arrives.

In those moments, the Essence, the Buddhata, escapes from within the intellect. Then, while in the absence of the "I" it experiences "That" which does not belong to time...

"That" is the Satori, the ecstasy of Saints, the Samadhi. In those moments, we can experience the Reality, the Truth.

It is necessary to use in our Gnostic lexicon the word Koan instead of the Chinese word Hua-tou, since the word Koan is now well-known and officially accepted in the West. Therefore, the word Koan as well as Hua-tou are respectively used in their general and specific sense.

In the aged country China, the Zen (Ch'an) Buddhists do not utilize the term Koan. They prefer to say, "Hua-tou exercise."

A monk asked Master Chao Chou, "Does a dog have Buddha nature?"

The Master answered, "Wu" (no). This single word "Wu," besides being a mantra that is pronounced as a double "u" like imitating the sound of a hurricane, is also a Koan itself.

To work with the Koan "Wu" while having the mind still and in silence, is something marvellous.

The experience of the "illuminating Void" allows us to experience an element that radically transforms.

Final Salutations

Beloved ones,

We have concluded the present 1969-1970 Christmas Message.

This is another book of the Fifth Gospel. Study and live it.

I want to tell you that these teachings for the New Aquarian Era are being delivered in accordance with the Law of Musical Octaves.

Each one of the books is developed in succesively higher notes. Therefore, when we will arrive at the note-synthesis, the message shall be concluded.

Afterwards, at that time, I will depart with my Divine Mother Kundalini towards Eternity.

Friends of mine, I beg you in a very dear way, do not send me through the mail or though any other way either praises, adulation, or flattery. Any letter carrying such vanities will be immediately sent back.

It is not enough to read this book: it is necessary to very profoundly study it, and to put these teachings into practice.

It is indispensable to leave the lukewarm state and to decide once and for all to tread the Path of the Razor's Edge.

Friends of mine, I wish for you a Merry Christmas and a prosperous new year. May the Star of Bethlehem shine on your path.

Inverential peace,

Samael Aun Weor

AMITABHA BUDDHA

Epilogue

We, the Adepts who have completed the Great Work, have the opportunity of splendidly manifesting the power of ubiquity. Thus, as an example, I can live here in this western world while simultaneously making myself visible and tangible in Tibet, guiding caravans throughout the Himalayas, etc.

All of these things are known in our Monastery, geographically situated or located at the right of the sacred valley of Amitabha.

I am an Adept of the White Fraternity, as is any individual from the Conscious Circle of the Solar Humanity who, as an Initiate, has reached the stature of an authentic, real Human Being. Undoubtedly, degrees of perfection of the Adept exist, since, indeed, one thing is to reach Adepthood, while a very different matter is to reach perfection in Adepthood. Many Initiates have reached Adepthood; however, the Adepts who have reached perfection in Adepthood are very rare.

A Superman is an Initiate who has reached perfection in Adepthood, one who has integrated himself with Divinity. This is how the Superman has to be understood.

So, there are degrees and degrees in everything, and different levels of the Being. Above us exists a superior level of the Being, and below us an inferior level of the Being. We can pass into another superior level only by eliminating a certain quantity of undesirable psychic aggregates (defects), which we carry within our interior. Obviously, only in this way is it possible to reach the highest level of the Being in order to transform ourselves into Supermen.

Let us then distinguish between an Adept who has already reached the level of Superman with another who has yet to reach it. This is the distinction that exists among the different Adepts of the Conscious Circle of the Solar Humanity.

Let it be understood that the authentic Superman is the Divinity inside a man. Therefore, what counts in us is the Being.

When the Being has totally integrated Himself within the Adept, then, we have the Superman.

I possess a living body in Egypt (in the state of catalepsy). Therefore, with such a situation I clearly enjoy immortality. I am not the only one who possesses immortality, for many other Egyptian Priests also have their physical bodies mummified in the Valley of the Kings. That is to say, there exists a group of Major Brethren who also have left their bodies in a state of catalepsy. Hence, such bodies, even now, are alive, and my case is one of them...

That is the only physical body that I had in Egypt during the dynasty of the Pharaoh Kephren. In my present existence, this mummy is useful because, by means of a constant atomic interchange, I will totally possess it. This signifies that I will continue to exist in this world with such a mummy.

I was reincarnated in China in the personality of Chou-Li. I also had other personalities, so I had many reincarnations in ancient China.

The most useful reincarnation among all was the one that I had as Julius Caesar, because I established the scenario for the development of the Fourth Subrace of this Fifth Aryan Root Race.

Indeed, the degree of Lama belongs to my Being. Undoubtedly, in ancient times I reincarnated in Tibet, at which time I received the degree of Lama. Many centuries have passed, and even in spite of having lost that Tibetan physical body, my interior, profound Being continues to be a Tibetan Lama. It is obvious that as Spirit, as Being, I always attend the reunions of the Sacred Order of Tibet.

The Sacred Order of Tibet is an organisation of sacred individuals. The Order is formed by 201 members, and the Major Rank is formed by 72 Brahmans. We possess the great Treasury of Aryavarta Ashram. Therefore, by all means, we can deduce with complete meridian clarity that the most exalted members of the Order are individuals who possess the Philosophical Stone.

The most elevated dignitary, the most exalted, is Bhagavan Aklaiva. He is the supreme director of the Sacred Order of Tibet.

We have had many Dalai Lamas. Presently, we have the fourteenth one, who, indeed, had to depart towards the sacred lands of India. He had to promptly leave from Tibet when the Communist Chinese hordes invaded the Tibetan land. He had no other choice but to escape to India, otherwise he would have been assassinated. The Dalai Lama is an Adept who works for humanity. However, as I previously stated, there have been many Dalai Lamas, and they will continue to exist in the future. Anyone who is a true reincarnation can convert himself into a Dalai Lama if this is what the Law wants. Not all the Dalai Lamas have reached total integration with Divinity. Nonetheless, all the Dalai Lamas are true Adepts in the most complete sense of the word.

Inevitably, the Communist Chinese will have to leave Tibet. Precisely the Dharmapalas, or legion of great Masters of Strength, are intensely working in order to eject the Chinese Communists from Tibet. They will leave after having suffered very much and when this happens, the Dalai Lama will again be placed on his throne.

Not all the Lamas are solar beings, only the ones who have performed the Great Work.

Some Lamas possess interplanetary ships, but this is only a very select group who live in the Himalayas, only this group and no other. They have their ships in inaccessible places, not only for the Tibetans, but also for the Chinese. It is very difficult to reach the place where these interplanetary ships exist.

The Masters of the great Aryan race live in Shangri La. They live within those caverns of Shangri La, along with Melchisedek (Keb), the king of the world.

Some secret apparatuses from ancient Atlantis still exist and are found within the caverns of Tibet and elsewhere. It is here in Tibet where a group of Lamas await me. Logically I will go there, after having accomplished my mission. I will secretly penetrate into Tibet.

Appendix

Excerpted from The Flying Saucer Conspiracy
by Major Donald E. Keyhoe, 1955
Chapter 5: Enigma On The Moon

On the night of July 29, 1953, John J. O'Neill, science editor
of the Herald Tribune, settled himself at his telescope for an
evening's observation of the moon. It was 6:30 U.T., and the
moon, on its northerly course, was approaching the equator
when O'Neill made an amazing discovery.

Streching above the Mare Crisium crater was a gigantic
bridge!

For a moment O'Neill refused to believe his senses. It
might be an optical illusion. With utmost care he rechecked
his telescope. He was using a 90X eyepiece. The "seeing"—an
Astronomer's term for visual conditions—was excellent.

He took another look.

The bridge was still there. Streching in a straight line from
pediment to pediment, it was more than 12 miles long.

The thing seemed impossible. In all the years he had watched
the moon, there had been no bridge — nothing at all — above the
Mare Crisium.

But there it was.

Fasinated, O'Neill watched the mysterious bridge for an
hour and a half. Twice he changed eyepieces, to a 125X and 250X.
Both times, under the higher magnification, the huge structure
appeared sharply in outline, an unbelievable engineering marvel
apparently erected in weeks, perhaps days.

Knowing the furor it would cause among astronomers, a
man with no less courage would have kept silent. As it was, not
even O'Neill dared to tell the whole story. In his report to the
Association of Lunar and Planetary Observers, he called his
discovery a "gigantic natural bridge." But the sudden appearance

of such a structure by an act of nature was absolutely impossible, as many privately admitted.

As O'Neill expected, he was quickly attacked by some astronomers. But most critics were abruptly silenced. For in August, 1953, one month after O'Neill's discovery, the existence of the bridge was fully confirmed by the great British astronomer, Dr. H.P. Wilkins. The following month it was also reported by another English lunar authority, Patrick Moore, a leading member of the British Astronomical Association.

The courage shown by O'Neill, Wilkins, and Moore soon led several astronomers to speak out on other moon mysteries-especially the strange lights so frequently seen in some craters.

On September 16, 1953, a peculiar, bright flash was seen on the moon by Rudolph M. Lippert, a member of the Lunar Section of the British Astronomical Association. Through his eight-inch Cassegrain reflector, with 90X power, the mysterious light glowed a yellowish orange, as bright as a first-magnitude star. Like the previous reports of strange lights, this was quickly explained away by more skeptical astronomers, who claimed it was a meteor hitting the moon.

But there was no way to brush off the Mare Crisium bridge discovery.

In public Dr. Wilkins, like O'Neill, had called it a strange "natural bridge." But his private comments had astonished members of the Royal Astronomical Association and the British Interplanetary Society.

It was not long before word of his comments reached the Pentagon. There the silence group learned with alarm that Wilkins was planning to make public his opinion of the bridge.

There was no way for the Pentagon censors to muzzle a British subject. All they could do was to pray the censors in London would somehow keep him from talking.

As I puzzled over the question of a moon base, I vaguely remembered some of the earlier recorded observations of the moon.

Within a short time, after I had talked with astronomers and searched astronomy records, a startling picture began to emerge.

For almost 200 years astronomers had watched mysterious activities on the moon.

Early in the nineteenth century Sir John Herschel, one of England's great astronomers, reported seeing strange, bright lights when the moon was darkened by an eclipse. Some of the lights, he said, seemed to be moving "above the moon."

Later, startling geometrical patterns resembling city streets were seen by the astronomer Gruithuisen.

In 1869 a sudden eruption of mystery lights, in regular patterns,caused a three-year investigation by the Royal Astronomical Society of Great Britain. Most of these puzzling lights were seen in the Mare Crisium area, where the gigantic bridge was later discovered. Watched by dozens of astronomers, the lights appeared in circular groups, triangular formations, and straight lines, their intensity varying as if by intelligent control.

Though the Royal Astronomical Society would not admit it publicly, some of its members believed this was an attempt by an unknown race on the moon to signal the earth. Until 1871 careful records were made every night, in the hope of deciphering the messages. Then, after nearly 2000 observations, the strange lights ceased to appear. If they were signals, their meaning was still a riddle.

Beside the puzzling lights, several mysterious dark objects had been sighted moving over the moon's surface. In 1912 Dr. F.B. Harris picked up a huge black object with his telescope. Estimated to be at least 50 miles across, it was clearly visible as it traversed the shinning face of the moon.

Since 1915 straight and curving walls had suddenly appeared in several craters, among them Archimedes and Aristarchus.

On March 30, 1950, Dr. H.P. Wilkins, using a 15 1/4-inch reflector, picked up a wierd glow in the Aristarchus-Herodotus region. Oval-shaped and strangely brilliant, it apparently came from some type of glowing machine hovering near the crater floor.

Three months later an almost identical light was sighted at the same spot by an experienced American astronomer, James C. Bartlett, Jr.

Most recent of all were the mystifying white "domes"- strange round formations, which appeared abruptly in many of the moon's craters.

All the evidence suggested not only the existence of a moon base, but that operations by an intelligent race had already begun. If so, who could the creatures be? Were they from other planets or did they originate on the moon?

Index

Blasphemous 181
Blavastsky, H.P. 69, 77
Blind 62, 137, 221
Bliss 150, 161
Blissful 96
Blood 171, 198-199, 248
Blue 79-81, 85, 108-109, 143, 209
Bluish 12, 152
Boar 105, 107
Boat 52, 64, 76, 82-83, 109, 129, 156-
      157, 176, 180, 193-194
Boat of Khepera 157
Boats 194
Bodhisattva 17-18, 173, 195-196, 251
Bodhisattva of Samael 195
Bodhisattvas 18, 173
Bodies 16, 46, 49, 59, 77, 79, 113,
      115, 119, 144-146, 168-169,
      178, 206, 210, 216-217, 233,
      235, 247, 256
Body of Conscious Will 168
Bohemia 224
Bohemian 111
Bolivar 12
Bolivia 46
Bomb 8, 23, 151
Bombing 187
Bombs 5, 171, 187-189
Bone 31, 140
Bones 31, 78, 135-136, 222, 235, 243
Book 12, 46, 59, 65-67, 77, 85, 87, 89,
      106, 112, 127, 129, 144-145,
      155-157, 163, 166, 173, 178-
      180, 186, 193-194, 197, 204-
      205, 215, 229, 239-240, 253
Book of Enoch 215
Book of Life 46, 59, 145, 178, 197
Books 67, 213, 253
Boreas 177
Born 21, 29, 35, 47, 68, 102, 105, 145-
      146, 165-167, 169-171, 175,
      182, 185, 219, 238, 245
Bosphorus 175
Bottled 92-93, 127, 132, 143, 168,
      210, 221
Boulders 63
Brahma 1, 3, 37, 69, 228-229

Brahma-Viraj 195
Brahmana 67
Brahmanism 27, 215
Brahmans 27, 67, 256
Brain 15, 139-141, 221
Brains 189
Brasit 69
Bread 81, 83
Breath 30, 103, 108, 141, 181
Breathe 79
Breathed 3
Breathes 14, 21, 53
Breathless 3, 53
Breaths 215
Brethren 29, 114-116, 133, 181, 256
Bretons 176
Bride 143
Britain 261
British 15, 72, 260
British Astronomical Association
      260
British Interplanetary Society 260
Brittanys 176
Bronze 62, 223
Bronzed 111
Brothels 101
Brother 13, 62, 129, 201
Brotherhood 52, 183, 224, 239
Bruno 36
Brutus 12, 35
Buddha 83, 94, 155, 162, 173, 180,
      207, 241, 251-252, 254
Buddha Shakyamuni 162
Buddhas 94
Buddhata 143, 252
Buddhi 17, 192
Buddhic 183
Buddhist 68, 92, 131-132, 149, 195,
      238-239, 251
Buddhist Aunad-Ad 195
Buddhist Aunadad-Ad 68
Buddhist Pratimoksha 238-239
Buddhist Satori 132
Buddhists 251-252
Build 97, 156, 167-168, 178, 206, 235
Built 168-169, 175, 183, 196, 216,
      235

Tsunamis 189
Tuathas of Danand 176
Tucumari 153
Tule 96
TUM 50, 63-64, 89
Tumor 202
Tumors 199, 202
Tung 251
Tunic 62-63, 179
Tunics 33, 113, 133
Twelve 7-9, 13, 15, 86, 184, 241-242
Twelve Nidanas 184, 241-242
Twenty 119
Twenty-eight 119, 136
Twenty-four 71
Twenty-one 41, 73-74
Twenty-six 163
Twice 35, 169, 182, 259
Twice Born 35, 77, 169, 182
Twilight 84, 130, 198
Twin 192, 248
Two 10, 13, 19, 21, 28-29, 31, 52,
        63, 71, 73-74, 87, 91, 99,
        113, 120, 132-133, 140-141,
        149, 152, 155, 160, 163, 174,
        185, 206, 220, 222, 227, 243,
        246-248
Two Truths 246
Tyranny 159
Tyrians 99-100, 175, 189
U. S. A. 86-87, 189, 214
Ubiquity 255
Uchikoshi 47
UFOs 5, 85-86
Ulcers 137
Ultrasonic 10
Ultraviolet 56-57, 121
Ulysses 12
Unconditioned 67, 117, 160
Unconscious 17, 147, 149, 217
Unconscious Itself 147, 149
Unconsciously 116
Unconsciousness 18, 147, 150, 221
Uncreated 1, 37, 39, 84, 133, 147,
        197, 227
Uncreated Light 1, 37, 39, 84, 133,
        147, 197, 227

Undefinable 83
Undefined 14, 123
Understand 47, 66-68, 83, 94, 111,
        127, 143, 150, 165, 179, 182,
        193, 200, 207, 219, 225, 233
Understanding 38, 167, 251
Understands 12
Understood 35, 81, 89, 160, 173, 182,
        224, 247, 255
Undifferentiated 3
Unfolded 29
Unfolding 195
Unfolds 11, 160, 200, 229
Union 201
Unique 3, 9, 65, 72, 116, 125, 140,
        207, 216, 229-230
Unique Divinity 65
Unique One 3, 65, 68, 195
UNIQUE-BEING 98, 186
United 6, 28-29, 87, 159, 187, 243
United States of America 6, 187
Unity 8, 21, 25, 37, 159, 237, 251
Universal 3, 33, 35, 37-39, 44, 57,
        121, 147, 150, 155, 175, 220
Universal Father 220
Universal Life 35, 44, 57
Universal Logos of Life 155
Universal Spirit of Life 3, 37, 147,
        150
Universe 1, 3, 6, 21, 37, 39, 52, 67-68,
        73, 84, 97-98, 117, 121, 124-
        125, 131-133, 145, 147, 149,
        153, 155, 160-161, 185, 229,
        235, 248
Universes 1, 3, 13, 23
University 56, 151, 202
University of Berkeley 56
University of New Mexico 151
Unknowable 21, 52, 68, 123, 179,
        227, 229, 233
Unknown 85, 189, 224, 261
Unknown Flying Objects 85
Unmanifested 1, 21, 106, 147
Unmanifested Absolute 21, 147
Unmanifested One 1
Upper-Individuality 211
Upright 27, 93, 100, 127

Books by the Same Author

Aquarian Message
Aztec Christic Magic
Book of the Dead
Book of the Virgin of Carmen
Buddha's Necklace
Christ Will
Christmas Messages (various)
Cosmic Ships
Cosmic Teachings of a Lama
Didactic Self-Knowledge
Dream Yoga (collected writings)
Elimination of Satan's Tail
Esoteric Course of Runic Magic
Esoteric Treatise of Hermetic Astrology
Esoteric Treatise of Theurgy
Fundamental Education
Fundamental Notions of Endocrinology
Gnostic Anthropology
Gnostic Catechism
The Great Rebellion
Greater Mysteries
Igneous Rose
The Initiatic Path in the Arcana of Tarot
    and Kabbalah

Introduction to Gnosis
Kabbalah of the Mayan Mysteries
Lamasery Exercises
Logos Mantra Theurgy
Manual of Practical Magic
Mysteries of Fire: Kundalini Yoga
Mystery of the Golden Blossom
Occult Medicine & Practical Magic
Parsifal Unveiled
The Perfect Matrimony
Pistis Sophia Unveiled
Revolution of Beelzebub
Revolution of the Dialectic
Revolutionary Psychology
Secret Doctrine of Anahuac
Three Mountains
Transmutation of Sexual Energy
Treatise of Sexual Alchemy
Yellow Book
Yes, There is Hell, a Devil, and Karma
Zodiacal Course
150 Answers from Master Samael Aun Weor

To learn more about Gnosis, visit gnosticteachings.org.

Thelema Press is a non-profit publisher dedicated to spreading the sacred universal doctrine to suffering humanity. All of our works are made possible by the kindness and generosity of sponsors. If you would like to make a tax-deductible donation, you may send it to the address below, or visit our website for other alternatives. If you would like to sponsor the publication of a book, please contact us at 212-501-6106 or help@gnosticteachings.org.

Thelema Press
PMB 192, 18645 SW Farmington Rd., Aloha OR 97007 USA
Phone: 212-501-6106 · Fax: 212-501-1676

Visit us online at:
gnosticteachings.org
gnosticradio.org
gnosticschool.org
gnosticstore.org
gnosticvideos.org